The
Overcomer's
Scripture Keys
From
A to Z

The Overcomer's Scripture Keys From A to Z

Scriptures for Winning Over Life's Problems

Kate McVeigh

This

*The Overcomer's Scripture Keys
From A to Z*

Presented to

_____

_____

By

_____

_____

Date

_____

_____

The Overcomer's Scripture Keys From A to Z
ISBN 0-9666940-0-7
Copyright © 1999 by Kate McVeigh

Kate McVeigh Ministries
P.O. Box 1688
Warren, MI 48090

3rd Printing

Editorial Consultant: Cynthia Hansen
Text/Cover Design: Kimberly M. Maskrey

CONTENTS

INTRODUCTION

Do you want to be a overcomer in life? Then you better start thinking and talking like one! A person who receives God's best in life is someone who goes around speaking words of faith all the time!

Check it out. People who go from failure to failure in their lives are people who consistently say the wrong things. They say they can't pay their bills — and they can't. They say they can't stop their bad habit, so they never do.

Jesus said in Mark 11:23 that you can have whatever you say. If you say God's Word won't work for you, it won't. But if you begin to confess what God says about you, it will eventually change you from a failure to an overcomer in life!

This is the revelation that changed my life. When I received Jesus as a sixteen-year-old girl, I had some big difficulties to overcome. You see, I had been placed in classes for slow learners since the fifth grade and had developed a very poor self-image. I was full of fears and insecurities.

But thank God for the life-changing power of His Word! My life completely changed as I began to confess God's Word and talk like an overcomer. For instance, I continually confessed that the Greater One lived in me and that I could do anything God had called me to do (1 John 4:4; Phil. 4:13).

My life is a living testimony to what believing and speaking God's Word can do. Before I was saved, I was absolutely terrified of getting up in front of my class to give a speech. Now God has made me a Bible teacher!

You see, as you faithfully meditate on God's Word and confess His promises with your mouth, the power of God turns your greatest weaknesses into your greatest strengths!

That's why I feel this book is so important. Within these pages are scriptural keys from A to Z that can take you from defeat to victory in every area of life. But it doesn't just happen automatically. It's up to you to:

- *Meditate* on the scriptures until they are planted deep in your heart.
- *Confess* what God says about you on a daily basis.
- *Apply* the truths that you learn from the Word to your life.

Such potential greatness lies ahead in your walk with God. You have the ability to literally see your circumstances transformed before your eyes as you release your faith in God's promises.

God has sent the Greater One to live on the inside of you. He has made you more than a conqueror through Jesus Christ (Rom. 8:37). So refuse to let the devil intimidate you. Start thinking, talking, and acting like the overcomer that God says you are. You *can* do all things through Christ!

A

ADDICTION

*Compulsive physiological necessity
for a habit-forming substance.*

NEW TESTAMENT

PHILIPPIANS 4:13

13 I can do all things through Christ which strength-
eneth me.

MATTHEW 8:2,3 (*NIV*)

2 A man with leprosy came and knelt before him
[Jesus] and said, "Lord, if you are willing, you
can make me clean."
3 Jesus reached out his hand and touched the
man. "I am willing," he said. "Be clean!" Immediately he was cured of his leprosy.

2 CORINTHIANS 3:4,5 (*Amplified*)

4 Such is the reliance and confidence that we
have through Christ toward and with reference
to God.
5 Not that we are fit (qualified and sufficient in
ability) of ourselves to form personal judg-
ments or to claim or count anything as coming

from us, but our power and ability and sufficiency are from God.

JOHN 15:4,5

4   Abide in me, and I in you. As the branch cannot bear fruit of itself, except it abide in the vine; no more can ye, except ye abide in me.
5   I am the vine, ye are the branches: He that abideth in me, and I in him, the same bringeth forth much fruit: for without me ye can do nothing.

2 CORINTHIANS 12:9,10

9   And he said unto me, My grace is sufficient for thee: for my strength is made perfect in weakness. Most gladly therefore will I rather glory in my infirmities, that the power of Christ may rest upon me.
10   Therefore I take pleasure in infirmities, in reproaches, in necessities, in persecutions, in distresses for Christ's sake: for when I am weak, then am I strong.

OLD TESTAMENT

ISAIAH 40:29-31

29   He giveth power to the faint; and to them that have no might he increaseth strength.

30 Even the youths shall faint and be weary, and the young men shall utterly fall:

31 But they that wait upon the Lord shall renew their strength; they shall mount up with wings as eagles; they shall run, and not be weary; and they shall walk, and not faint.

ISAIAH 41:10

10 Fear thou not; for I am with thee: be not dismayed; for I am thy God: I will strengthen thee; yea, I will help thee; yea, I will uphold thee with the right hand of my righteousness.

Overcomer's Confession:

I am delivered by the blood of Jesus. Sin has no power over me — I am free in Jesus' Name!

ANGER

A strong emotion of resentment or animosity.

NEW TESTAMENT

EPHESIANS 4:26

26 Be ye angry, and sin not: let not the sun go down upon your wrath.

EPHESIANS 4:26 (*Amplified*)

26 When angry, do not sin; do not ever let your wrath (your exasperation, your fury or indignation) last until the sun goes down.

EPHESIANS 4:31 (*Amplified*)

31 Let all bitterness and indignation and wrath (passion, rage, bad temper) and resentment (anger, animosity) and quarreling (brawling, clamor, contention) and slander (evil-speaking, abusive or blasphemous language) be banished from you, with all malice (spite, ill will, or baseness of any kind).

MATTHEW 5:22-24

22 But I say unto you, That whosoever is angry with his brother without a cause shall be in danger of the judgment: and whosoever shall say to his brother, Raca,* shall be in danger of

* An Aramaic term of contempt.

the council: but whosoever shall say, Thou fool, shall be in danger of hell fire.

23 Therefore if thou bring thy gift to the altar, and there rememberest that thy brother hath ought against thee;

24 Leave there thy gift before the altar, and go thy way; first be reconciled to thy brother, and then come and offer thy gift.

TITUS 1:7 (*NIV*)

7 Since an overseer is entrusted with God's work, he must be blameless — not overbearing, not quick-tempered, not given to drunkenness, not violent, not pursuing dishonest gain.

GALATIANS 5:19-21 (*Amplified*)

19 Now the doings (practices) of the flesh are clear (obvious): they are immorality, impurity, indecency,

20 Idolatry, sorcery, enmity, strife, jealousy, anger (ill temper), selfishness, divisions (dissensions), party spirit (factions, sects with peculiar opinions, heresies),

21 Envy, drunkenness, carousing, and the like. I warn you beforehand, just as I did previously, that those who do such things shall not inherit the kingdom of God.

EPHESIANS 6:4

4   And, ye fathers, provoke not your children to wrath: but bring them up in the nurture and admonition of the Lord.

COLOSSIANS 3:8 (*NIV*)

8   But now you must rid yourselves of all such things as these: anger, rage, malice, slander, and filthy language from your lips.

1 TIMOTHY 2:8 (*NIV*)

8   I want men everywhere to lift up holy hands in prayer, without anger or disputing.

JAMES 1:19,20 (*Amplified*)

19 Understand [this], my beloved brethren, Let every man be quick to hear [a ready listener], slow to speak, slow to take offense and to get angry.
20 For man's anger does not promote the righteousness God [wishes and requires].

OLD TESTAMENT

PROVERBS 15:18

18 A wrathful man stirreth up strife: but he that is slow to anger appeaseth strife.

PROVERBS 16:32

32 He that is slow to anger is better than the
mighty; and he that ruleth his spirit than he
that taketh a city.

Overcomer's Confession:

I do not let anger rule me — I rule *it*! Thank You,
Holy Spirit, for helping me control my feelings.

B

BEGUILE

To deceive by deception; defraud.

NEW TESTAMENT

COLOSSIANS 2:4-6

4 And this I say, lest any man should beguile you with enticing words.

5 For though I be absent in the flesh, yet am I with you in the spirit, joying and beholding your order, and the stedfastness of your faith in Christ.

6 As ye have therefore received Christ Jesus the Lord, so walk ye in him.

COLOSSIANS 2:18

18 Let no man beguile you of your reward in a voluntary humility and worshipping of angels, intruding into those things which he hath not seen, vainly puffed up by his fleshly mind.

COLOSSIANS 2:18 (*Amplified*)

18 Let no one defraud you by acting as an umpire and declaring you unworthy and disqualifying you for the prize, insisting on self-abasement and worship of angels, taking his stand on

9

visions [he claims] he has seen, vainly puffed up by his sensuous notions and inflated by his unspiritual thoughts and fleshly conceit.

ROMANS 16:17,18 (*NIV*)

17 I urge you, brothers, to watch out for those who cause divisions and put obstacles in your way that are contrary to the teaching you have learned. Keep away from them.

18 For such people are not serving our Lord Christ, but their own appetites. By smooth talk and flattery they deceive the minds of naive people.

1 CORINTHIANS 3:18,19

18 Let no man deceive himself. If any man among you seemeth to be wise in this world, let him become a fool, that he may be wise.

19 For the wisdom of this world is foolishness with God. For it is written, He taketh the wise in their own craftiness.

GALATIANS 6:3 (*Amplified*)

3 For if any person thinks himself to be somebody [too important to condescend to shoulder another's load] when he is nobody [of superiority except in his own estimation], he deceives and deludes and cheats himself.

GALATIANS 6:7 (*Amplified*)

7 Do not be deceived and deluded and misled; God will not allow Himself to be sneered at (scorned, disdained, or mocked by mere pretensions or professions, or by His precepts being set aside). [He inevitably deludes himself who attempts to delude God.] For whatever a man sows, that and that only is what he will reap.

JAMES 1:22

22 But be ye doers of the word, and not hearers only, deceiving your own selves.

JAMES 1:26

26 If any man among you seem to be religious, and bridleth not his tongue, but deceiveth his own heart, this man's religion is vain.

1 THESSALONIANS 4:6,7 (*Amplified*)

6 That no man transgress and overreach his brother and defraud him in this matter or defraud his brother in business. For the Lord is an avenger in all these things, as we have already warned you solemnly and told you plainly.

7 For God has not called us to impurity but to consecration [to dedicate ourselves to the most thorough purity].

OLD TESTAMENT

PROVERBS 24:28,29 (*NIV*)

28 Do not testify against your neighbor without cause, or use your lips to deceive.

29 Do not say, "I'll do to him as he has done to me; I'll pay that man back for what he did."

PROVERBS 26:18,19 (*NIV*)

18 Like a madman shooting firebrands or deadly arrows

19 is a man who deceives his neighbor and says, "I was only joking!"

Overcomer's Confession:

I never deceive or defraud others but always speak the truth in love. And because the Holy Spirit is my Teacher and Guide, I will not be deceived. I walk in the light of God's truth all the days of my life!

BITTERNESS

A sharp, ill-natured hostility, especially as it is exhibited in words or action.

NEW TESTAMENT

HEBREWS 12:14,15

14 Follow peace with all men, and holiness, without which no man shall see the Lord:

15 Looking diligently lest any man fail of the grace of God; lest any root of bitterness springing up trouble you, and thereby many be defiled.

ACTS 8:22,23 (*NIV*)

22 "Repent of this wickedness and pray to the Lord. Perhaps he will forgive you for having such a thought in your heart.

23 For I see that you are full of bitterness and captive to sin."

ROMANS 3:11-14

11 There is none that understandeth, there is none that seeketh after God.

12 They are all gone out of the way, they are together become unprofitable; there is none that doeth good, no, not one.

13 Their throat is an open sepulcher; with their tongues they have used deceit; the poison of asps is under their lips:

14 Whose mouth is full of cursing and bitterness.

EPHESIANS 4:30-32

30 And grieve not the holy Spirit of God, whereby ye are sealed unto the day of redemption.

31 Let all bitterness, and wrath, and anger, and clamour, and evil speaking, be put away from you, with all malice:

32 And be ye kind one to another, tenderhearted, forgiving one another, even as God for Christ's sake hath forgiven you.

OLD TESTAMENT

ISAIAH 38:16,17

16 O Lord, by these things men live, and in all these things is the life of my spirit: so wilt thou recover me, and make me to live.

17 Behold, for peace I had great bitterness: but thou hast in love to my soul delivered it from the pit of corruption: for thou hast cast all my sins behind thy back.

Overcomer's Confession:

I will not be bitter; I choose to forgive. God's love is working in me now.

BLAME

To hold accountable; to find fault with;
to condemn. Deserving condemnation; at fault.

NEW TESTAMENT

ROMANS 8:1

1 There is therefore now no condemnation to them which are in Christ Jesus, who walk not after the flesh, but after the Spirit.

EPHESIANS 1:3,4

3 Blessed be the God and Father of our Lord Jesus Christ, who hath blessed us with all spiritual blessings in heavenly places in Christ:

4 According as he hath chosen us in him before the foundation of the world, that we should be holy and without blame before him in love.

EPHESIANS 1:3,4 *(Amplified)*

3 May blessing (praise, laudation, and eulogy) be to the God and Father of our Lord Jesus Christ (the Messiah) Who has blessed us in Christ with every spiritual (given by the Holy Spirit) blessing in the heavenly realm!

4 Even as [in His love] He chose us [actually picked us out for Himself as His own] in Christ before the foundation of the world, that we

should be holy (consecrated and set apart for Him) and blameless in His sight, even above reproach, before Him in love.

JAMES 5:16

16 Confess your faults one to another, and pray one for another, that ye may be healed. The effectual fervent prayer of a righteous man availeth much.

JAMES 5:16 (*Amplified*)

16 Confess to one another therefore your faults (your slips, your false steps, your offenses, your sins) and pray [also] for one another, that you may be healed and restored [to a spiritual tone of mind and heart]. The earnest (heartfelt, continued) prayer of a righteous man makes tremendous power available [dynamic in its working].

1 CORINTHIANS 6:7,8

7 Now therefore there is utterly a fault among you, because ye go to law one with another. Why do ye not rather take wrong? why do ye not rather suffer yourselves to be defrauded?

8 Nay, ye do wrong, and defraud, and that your brethren.

GALATIANS 6:1

1 Brethren, if a man be overtaken in a fault, ye which are spiritual, restore such an one in the spirit of meekness; considering thyself, lest thou also be tempted.

MARK 7:1-3

1 Then came together unto him the Pharisees, and certain of the scribes, which came from Jerusalem.
2 And when they saw some of his disciples eat bread with defiled, that is to say, with unwashen, hands, they found fault.
3 For the Pharisees, and all the Jews, except they wash their hands oft, eat not, holding the tradition of the elders.

2 CORINTHIANS 6:3 (*Amplified*)

3 We put no obstruction in anybody's way [we give no offense in anything], so that no fault may be found and [our] ministry blamed and discredited.

PHILIPPIANS 2:14,15

14 Do all things without murmurings and disputings:
15 That ye may be blameless and harmless, the sons of God, without rebuke, in the midst of a

crooked and perverse nation, among whom ye shine as lights in the world.

2 PETER 3:14

14 Wherefore, beloved, seeing that ye look for such things, be diligent that ye may be found of him in peace, without spot, and blameless.

OLD TESTAMENT

JOB 1:22

22 In all this Job sinned not, nor charged God foolishly.

DANIEL 6:4

4 Then the presidents and princes sought to find occasion against Daniel concerning the kingdom; but they could find none occasion nor fault; forasmuch as he was faithful, neither was there any error or fault found in him.

Overcomer's Confession:

I will not blame others nor God for my problems. Only good comes from God. And because of the blood of Jesus, I stand blameless before Him!

C

CHARITY

*Generosity; provision of help or aid
to the poor; love.*

NEW TESTAMENT

1 CORINTHIANS 13:4-7

4 Charity suffereth long, and is kind; charity
envieth not; charity vaunteth not itself, is not
puffed up,
5 Doth not behave itself unseemly, seeketh not
her own, is not easily provoked, thinketh no
evil;
6 Rejoiceth not in iniquity, but rejoiceth in the
truth;
7 Beareth all things, believeth all things, hopeth
all things, endureth all things.

MATTHEW 5:42

42 Give to him that asketh thee, and from him
that would borrow of thee turn not thou away.

MATTHEW 19:21 (*Amplified*)

21 Jesus answered him, If you would be perfect
[that is, have that spiritual maturity which
accompanies self-sacrificing character], go and

sell what you have and give to the poor and you
will have riches in heaven; and come, be My
disciple [side with My party and follow Me].

MATTHEW 25:35 (*Amplified*)

35 For I was hungry and you gave Me food, I was
thirsty and you gave Me something to drink, I
was a stranger and you brought Me together
with yourselves and welcomed and entertained
and lodged Me.

MARK 9:41

41 For whosoever shall give you a cup of water to
drink in my name, because ye belong to Christ,
verily I say unto you, he shall not lose his
reward.

LUKE 3:11 (*NIV*)

11 John answered, "The man with two tunics
should share with him who has none, and the
one who has food should do the same."

ACTS 6:1-4

1 And in those days, when the number of the disciples was multiplied, there arose a murmuring
of the Grecians against the Hebrews, because
their widows were neglected in the daily ministration.

2 Then the twelve called the multitude of the disciples unto them, and said, It is not reason that we should leave the word of God, and serve tables.

3 Wherefore, brethren, look ye out among you seven men of honest report, full of the Holy Ghost and wisdom, whom we may appoint over this business.

4 But we will give ourselves continually to prayer, and to the ministry of the word.

ACTS 11:29,30

29 Then the disciples, every man according to his ability, determined to send relief unto the brethren which dwelt in Judaea:

30 Which also they did, and sent it to the elders by the hands of Barnabas and Saul.

ROMANS 15:25-27 (NIV)

25 Now, however, I am on my way to Jerusalem in the service of the saints there.

26 For Macedonia and Achaia were pleased to make a contribution for the poor among the saints in Jerusalem.

27 They were pleased to do it, and indeed they owe it to them. For if the Gentiles have shared in the Jews' spiritual blessings, they owe it to the Jews to share with them their material blessings.

COLOSSIANS 3:14

14 And above all these things put on charity, which is the bond of perfectness.

2 THESSALONIANS 1:3

3   We are bound to thank God always for you, brethren, as it is meet, because that your faith groweth exceedingly, and the charity of every one of you all toward each other aboundeth.

1 TIMOTHY 5:8

8   But if any provide not for his own, and specially for those of his own house, he hath denied the faith, and is worse than an infidel.

JAMES 2:15,16 (*NIV*)

15 Suppose a brother or sister is without clothes and daily food.
16 If one of you says to him, "Go, I wish you well; keep warm and well fed," but does nothing about his physical needs, what good is it?

1 PETER 4:8

8   And above all things have fervent charity among yourselves: for charity shall cover the multitude of sins.

1 JOHN 3:17 (*NIV*)

17 If anyone has material possessions and sees his brother in need but has no pity on him, how can the love of God be in him?

1 JOHN 3:18

18 My little children, let us not love in word, neither in tongue; but in deed and in truth.

Overcomer's Confession:

I show the love of God to others not only through my words but through my actions. I'm always looking for ways to be a blessing!

CHILDREN

A boy or girl from birth to adolescence;
a son or daughter.

NEW TESTAMENT

MATTHEW 18:10

10 Take heed that ye despise not one of these little
ones; for I say unto you, That in heaven their
angels do always behold the face of my Father
which is in heaven.

MATTHEW 15:4 (*Amplified*)

4   For God commanded, Honor your father and
your mother, and, He who curses or reviles or
speaks evil of or abuses or treats improperly his
father or mother, let him surely come to his end
by death.

EPHESIANS 6:1-4

1   Children, obey your parents in the Lord: for
this is right.
2   Honour thy father and mother; which is the
first commandment with promise;
3   That it may be well with thee, and thou mayest
live long on the earth.

4   And, ye fathers, provoke not your children to
     wrath: but bring them up in the nurture and
     admonition of the Lord.

OLD TESTAMENT

DEUTERONOMY 6:6,7

6   And these words, which I command thee this
     day, shall be in thine heart:
7   And thou shalt teach them diligently unto thy
     children, and shalt talk of them when thou
     sittest in thine house, and when thou walkest
     by the way, and when thou liest down, and
     when thou risest up.

PSALM 127:3-5

3   Lo, children are an heritage of the Lord: and
     the fruit of the womb is his reward.
4   As arrows are in the hand of a mighty man; so
     are children of the youth.
5   Happy is the man that hath his quiver full of
     them: they shall not be ashamed, but they
     shall speak with the enemies in the gate.

PROVERBS 13:1

1   A wise son heareth his father's instruction: but
     a scorner heareth not rebuke.

ISAIAH 54:13

13 And all thy children shall be taught of the Lord;
   and great shall be the peace of thy children.

ISAIAH 54:13 (*Amplified*)

13 And all your [spiritual] children shall be disciples [taught by the Lord and obedient to His
   will], and great shall be the peace and undisturbed composure of your children.

Overcomer's Confession:

My children are a blessing, taught of the Lord and
obedient to His will. Great is their peace and
undisturbed composure!

CONDEMNATION

*To declare to be guilty of wrongdoing;
to inflict a penalty upon.*

NEW TESTAMENT

ROMANS 8:1

1   There is therefore now no condemnation to them which are in Christ Jesus, who walk not after the flesh, but after the Spirit.

ROMANS 2:1

1   Therefore thou art inexcusable, O man, whosoever thou art that judgest: for wherein thou judgest another, thou condemnest thyself; for thou that judgest doest the same things.

MATTHEW 12:37

37 For by thy words thou shalt be justified, and by thy words thou shalt be condemned.

ROMANS 5:16 (*NIV*)

16 Again, the gift of God is not like the result of the one man's sin: The judgment followed one sin and brought condemnation, but the gift followed many trespasses and brought justification.

JOHN 3:17

17 For God sent not his Son into the world to condemn the world; but that the world through him might be saved.

LUKE 6:37

37 Judge not, and ye shall not be judged: condemn not, and ye shall not be condemned: forgive, and ye shall be forgiven.

1 JOHN 1:9

9 If we confess our sins, he is faithful and just to forgive us our sins, and to cleanse us from all unrighteousness.

1 JOHN 3:19-22 (*NIV*)

19 This then is how we know that we belong to the truth, and how we set our hearts at rest in his presence

20 whenever our hearts condemn us. For God is greater than our hearts, and he knows everything.

21 Dear friends, if our hearts do not condemn us, we have confidence before God

22 and receive from him anything we ask, because we obey his commands and do what pleases him.

OLD TESTAMENT

JOB 9:20

20 If I justify myself, mine own mouth shall condemn me: if I say, I am perfect, it shall also prove me perverse.

PSALM 37:32,33 (*NIV*)

32 The wicked lie in wait for the righteous, seeking their very lives;
33 but the Lord will not leave them in their power or let them be condemned when brought to trial.

PSALM 103:2-4

2 Bless the Lord, O my soul, and forget not all his benefits:
3 Who forgiveth all thine iniquities; who healeth all thy diseases;
4 Who redeemeth thy life from destruction; who crowneth thee with lovingkindness and tender mercies.

PROVERBS 12:2

2 A good man obtaineth favour of the Lord: but a man of wicked devices will he condemn.

ISAIAH 50:9

9   Behold, the Lord God will help me; who is he
    that shall condemn me? lo, they all shall wax
    old as a garment; the moth shall eat them up.

Overcomer's Confession:

My sins are washed away by the blood of Jesus, so
I'm free from condemnation. God doesn't remember
my sins anymore, and neither will I. I am forgiven!

D

DILIGENCE

*Fervent and enduring devotion to an endeavor;
steadfast effort; perseverance.*

NEW TESTAMENT

HEBREWS 11:6

6 But without faith it is impossible to please him:
for he that cometh to God must believe that he
is, and that he is a rewarder of them that diligently seek him.

PHILIPPIANS 3:13,14

13 Brethren, I count not myself to have appre-
hended: but this one thing I do, forgetting
those things which are behind, and reaching
forth unto those things which are before,
14 I press toward the mark for the prize of the
high calling of God in Christ Jesus.

2 PETER 1:5-8,10

5 And beside this, giving all diligence, add to
your faith virtue; and to virtue knowledge;
6 And to knowledge temperance; and to temperance patience; and to patience godliness;

7   And to godliness brotherly kindness; and to
     brotherly kindness charity.
8   For if these things be in you, and abound, they
     make you that ye shall neither be barren nor
     unfruitful in the knowledge of our Lord Jesus
     Christ . . . .
10   Wherefore the rather, brethren, give diligence
     to make your calling and election sure: for if ye
     do these things, ye shall never fall.

HEBREWS 6:10-12

10   For God is not unrighteous to forget your work
     and labour of love, which ye have shewed
     toward his name, in that ye have ministered to
     the saints, and do minister.
11   And we desire that every one of you do shew
     the same diligence to the full assurance of hope
     unto the end:
12   That ye be not slothful, but followers of them
     who through faith and patience inherit the
     promises.

GALATIANS 6:9

9   And let us not be weary in well doing: for in
     due season we shall reap, if we faint not.

OLD TESTAMENT

DEUTERONOMY 4:9

9 Only take heed to thyself, and keep thy soul diligently, lest thou forget the things which thine eyes have seen, and lest they depart from thy heart all the days of thy life: but teach them thy sons, and thy sons' sons.

DEUTERONOMY 6:17

17 Ye shall diligently keep the commandments of the Lord your God, and his testimonies, and his statutes, which he hath commanded thee.

DEUTERONOMY 11:13-15

13 And it shall come to pass, if ye shall hearken diligently unto my commandments which I command you this day, to love the Lord your God, and to serve him with all your heart and with all your soul,

14 That I will give you the rain of your land in his due season, the first rain and the latter rain, that thou mayest gather in thy corn, and thy wine, and thine oil.

15 And I will send grass in thy fields for thy cattle, that thou mayest eat and be full.

PROVERBS 4:23

23 Keep thy heart with all diligence; for out of it are the issues of life.

PROVERBS 10:4

4 He becometh poor that dealeth with a slack hand: but the hand of the diligent maketh rich.

Overcomer's Confession:

I am seeking God diligently, and He is blessing me. I will not grow weary as I obey His Word and serve Him with all my heart!

DISCOURAGEMENT

The condition of being deprived of courage,
hope, or confidence.

NEW TESTAMENT:

JOHN 16:33

33 These things I have spoken unto you, that in
me ye might have peace. In the world ye shall
have tribulation: but be of good cheer; I have
overcome the world.

JOHN 16:33 (*Amplified*)

33 I have told you these things, so that in Me you
may have [perfect] peace and confidence. In the
world you have tribulation and trials and distress
and frustration; but be of good cheer [take
courage; be confident, certain, undaunted]! For I
have overcome the world. [I have deprived it of
power to harm you and have conquered it for
you.]

HEBREWS 12:12,13

12 Wherefore lift up the hands which hang down,
and the feeble knees;
13 And make straight paths for your feet, lest that
which is lame be turned out of the way; but let
it rather be healed.

ACTS 14:21,22 (*Amplified*)

21 When they [Paul and Barnabus] had preached the good news (Gospel) to that town and made disciples of many of the people, they went back to Lystra and Iconium and Antioch.

22 Establishing and strengthening the souls and the hearts of the disciples, urging and warning and encouraging them to stand firm in the faith, and [telling them] that it is through many hardships and tribulations we must enter the kingdom of God.

ROMANS 8:18

18 For I reckon that the sufferings of this present time are not worthy to be compared with the glory which shall be revealed in us.

2 CORINTHIANS 4:17,18

17 For our light affliction, which is but for a moment, worketh for us a far more exceeding and eternal weight of glory,

18 While we look not at the things which are seen, but at the things which are not seen: for the things which are seen are temporal; but the things which are not seen are eternal.

JOHN 16:19,20

19 Now Jesus knew that they were desirous to ask him, and said unto them, Do ye inquire among

yourselves of that I said, A little while, and ye shall not see me: and again, a little while, and ye shall see me?

20 Verily, verily, I say unto you, That ye shall weep and lament, but the world shall rejoice: and ye shall be sorrowful, but your sorrow shall be turned into joy.

2 TIMOTHY 3:11,12

11 Persecutions, afflictions, which came unto me at Antioch, at Iconium, at Lystra; what persecutions I endured: but out of them all the Lord delivered me.

12 Yea, and all that will live godly in Christ Jesus shall suffer persecution.

OLD TESTAMENT

NUMBERS 32:9-11

9 For when they [the ten unbelieving spies] went up unto the valley of Eshcol, and saw the land, they discouraged the heart of the children of Israel, that they should not go into the land which the Lord had given them.

10 And the Lord's anger was kindled the same time, and he sware, saying,

11 Surely none of the men that came up out of Egypt, from twenty years old and upward, shall see the land which I sware unto Abraham, unto

Isaac, and unto Jacob; because they have not wholly followed me.

DEUTERONOMY 1:21

21 Behold, the Lord thy God hath set the land before thee: go up and possess it, as the Lord God of thy fathers hath said unto thee; fear not, neither be discouraged.

PROVERBS 13:12 (*NIV*)

12 Hope deferred makes the heart sick, but a longing fulfilled is a tree of life.

PSALM 42:11

11 Why art thou cast down, O my soul? and why art thou disquieted within me? hope thou in God: for I shall yet praise him, who is the health of my countenance, and my God.

Overcomer's Confession:

I refuse to be discouraged because God is on my side!

DOUBT (*see* UNBELIEF)

Verb: *To be undecided or skeptical about; distrust.*

Noun: *A lack of certainty or trust that often leads to irresolution; the condition of being unsettled or unresolved.*

NEW TESTAMENT

MARK 11:23

23 For verily I say unto you, That whosoever shall say unto this mountain, Be thou removed, and be thou cast into the sea; and shall not doubt in his heart, but shall believe that those things which he saith shall come to pass; he shall have whatsoever he saith.

ROMANS 4:16-21 (*NIV*)

16 Therefore, the promise comes by faith, so that it may be by grace and may be guaranteed to all Abraham's offspring — not only to those who are of the law but also to those who are of the faith of Abraham. He is the father of us all.

17 As it is written: "I have made you a father of many nations." He is our father in the sight of God, in whom he believed — the God who gives life to the dead and calls things that are not as though they were.

18 Against all hope, Abraham in hope believed and so became the father of many nations, just as it had been said to him, "So shall your off-spring be."
19 Without weakening in his faith, he faced the fact that his body was as good as dead — since he was about a hundred years old — and that Sarah's womb was also dead.
20 Yet he did not waver through unbelief regarding the promise of God, but was strengthened in his faith and gave glory to God,
21 being fully persuaded that God had power to do what he had promised.

ROMANS 14:20-23 (*NIV*)

20 Do not destroy the work of God for the sake of food. All food is clean, but it is wrong for a man to eat anything that causes someone else to stumble.
21 It is better not to eat meat or drink wine or to do anything else that will cause your brother to fall.
22 So whatever you believe about these things keep between yourself and God. Blessed is the man who does not condemn himself by what he approves.
23 But the man who has doubts is condemned if he eats, because his eating is not from faith; and everything that does not come from faith is sin.

JAMES 1:5-8

5 If any of you lack wisdom, let him ask of God,
   that giveth to all men liberally, and upbraideth
   not; and it shall be given him.
6 But let him ask in faith, nothing wavering. For
   he that wavereth is like a wave of the sea
   driven with the wind and tossed.
7 For let not that man think that he shall receive
   any thing of the Lord.
8 A double minded man is unstable in all his
   ways.

OLD TESTAMENT

NUMBERS 11:21-23

21 And Moses said, The people, among whom I
    am, are six hundred thousand footmen; and
    thou hast said, I will give them flesh, that they
    may eat a whole month.
22 Shall the flocks and the herds be slain for
    them, to suffice them? or shall all the fish of
    the sea be gathered together for them, to suf-
    fice them?
23 And the Lord said unto Moses, Is the Lord's
    hand waxed short? thou shalt see now whether
    my word shall come to pass unto thee or not.

NUMBERS 20:12

12 And the Lord spake unto Moses and Aaron,
    Because ye believed me not, to sanctify me in

the eyes of the children of Israel, therefore ye shall not bring this congregation into the land which I have given them.

PSALM 78:32

32 For all this they sinned still, and believed not for his wondrous works.

PSALM 95:7-11

7 For he is our God; and we are the people of his pasture, and the sheep of his hand. To day if ye will hear his voice,

8 Harden not your heart, as in the provocation, and as in the day of temptation in the wilderness:

9 When your fathers tempted me, proved me, and saw my work.

10 Forty years long was I grieved with this generation, and said, It is a people that do err in their heart, and they have not known my ways:

11 Unto whom I sware in my wrath that they should not enter into my rest.

Overcomer's Confession:

I am a believer, not a doubter. I believe; therefore, I receive!

E

ENDURANCE

The ability to last, continue, or remain even when suffering affliction, distress, or fatigue; fortitude.

NEW TESTAMENT

2 TIMOTHY 2:3

3 Thou therefore endure hardness, as a good soldier of Jesus Christ.

MATTHEW 10:22

22 And ye shall be hated of all men for my name's sake: but he that endureth to the end shall be saved.

ROMANS 12:12 (*Amplified*)

12 Rejoice and exult in hope; be steadfast and patient in suffering and tribulation; be constant in prayer.

2 TIMOTHY 2:10

10 Therefore I endure all things for the elect's sakes, that they may also obtain the salvation which is in Christ Jesus with eternal glory.

HEBREWS 12:2,3

2   Looking unto Jesus the author and finisher of our faith; who for the joy that was set before him endured the cross, despising the shame, and is set down at the right hand of the throne of God.

3   For consider him that endured such contradiction of sinners against himself, lest ye be wearied and faint in your minds.

HEBREWS 12:2,3 (*Amplified*)

2   Looking away [from all that will distract] to Jesus, Who is the Leader and the Source of our faith [giving the first incentive for our belief] and is also its Finisher [bringing it to maturity and perfection]. He, for the joy [of obtaining the prize] that was set before Him, endured the cross, despising and ignoring the shame, and is now seated at the right hand of the throne of God.

3   Just think of Him Who endured from sinners such grievous opposition and bitter hostility against Himself [reckon up and consider it all in comparison with your trials], so that you may not grow weary or exhausted, losing heart and relaxing and fainting in your minds.

HEBREWS 12:5-7 (*NIV*)

5   And you have forgotten that word of encouragement that addresses you as sons: "My son, do

not make light of the Lord's discipline, and do not lose heart when he rebukes you,

6 because the Lord disciplines those he loves, and he punishes everyone he accepts as a son."

7 Endure hardship as discipline; God is treating you as sons. For what son is not disciplined by his father?

JAMES 1:12 (*Amplified*)

12 Blessed (happy, to be envied) is the man who is patient under trial and stands up under temptation, for when he has stood the test and been approved, he will receive [the victor's] crown of life which God has promised to those who love Him.

OLD TESTAMENT

PSALM 30:5

5 For his anger endureth but a moment; in his favour is life: weeping may endure for a night, but joy cometh in the morning.

PSALM 72:17

17 His name shall endure for ever: his name shall be continued as long as the sun: and men shall be blessed in him: all nations shall call him blessed.

PSALM 107:1

1   O give thanks unto the Lord, for he is good: for his mercy endureth for ever.

PSALM 111:3

3   His work is honourable and glorious: and his righteousness endureth for ever.

PSALM 111:10

10 The fear of the Lord is the beginning of wisdom: a good understanding have all they that do his commandments: his praise endureth for ever.

Overcomer's Confession:

I will stand on the Word of God. I am not moved by what I hear, feel, or see. The Word is working mightily in me now!

F

FAITH

Confident belief in the truth, value, or trustworthiness of a person, an idea, or a thing.

Belief that does not rest on logical proof or material evidence.

NEW TESTAMENT

MARK 11:22-24

22 And Jesus answering saith unto them, Have faith in God.

23 For verily I say unto you, That whosoever shall say unto this mountain, Be thou removed, and be thou cast into the sea; and shall not doubt in his heart, but shall believe that those things which he saith shall come to pass; he shall have whatsoever he saith.

24 Therefore I say unto you, What things soever ye desire, when ye pray, believe that ye receive them, and ye shall have them.

HEBREWS 11:1

1 Now faith is the substance of things hoped for, the evidence of things not seen.

HEBREWS 11:1 (*Amplified*)

1   Now faith is the assurance (the confirmation, the title deed) of the things [we] hope for, being the proof of things [we] do not see and the conviction of their reality [faith perceiving as real fact what is not revealed to the senses].

HEBREWS 11:32-34

32   And what shall I more say? for the time would fail me to tell of Gedeon, and of Barak, and of Samson, and of Jephthae; of David also, and Samuel, and of the prophets:
33   Who through faith subdued kingdoms, wrought righteousness, obtained promises, stopped the mouths of lions,
34   Quenched the violence of fire, escaped the edge of the sword, out of weakness were made strong, waxed valiant in fight, turned to flight the armies of the aliens.

ROMANS 10:8-10

8   But what saith it? The word is nigh thee, even in thy mouth, and in thy heart; that is, the word of faith, which we preach;
9   That if thou shalt confess with thy mouth the Lord Jesus, and shalt believe in thine heart that God hath raised him from the dead, thou shalt be saved.

10 For with the heart man believeth unto righteousness; and with the mouth confession is made unto salvation.

ROMANS 10:17

17 So then faith cometh by hearing, and hearing by the word of God.

2 CORINTHIANS 4:13

13 We having the same spirit of faith, according as it is written, I believed, and therefore have I spoken; we also believe, and therefore speak.

2 CORINTHIANS 5:7 (*Amplified*)

7 For we walk by faith [we regulate our lives and conduct ourselves by our conviction or belief respecting man's relationship to God and divine things, with trust and holy fervor; thus we walk] not by sight or appearance.

1 TIMOTHY 6:12

12 Fight the good fight of faith, lay hold on eternal life, whereunto thou art also called, and hast professed a good profession before many witnesses.

JAMES 2:17-23 (*NIV*)

17 In the same way, faith by itself, if it is not accompanied by action, is dead.

18 But someone will say, "You have faith; I have deeds." Show me your faith without deeds, and I will show you my faith by what I do.

19 You believe that there is one God. Good! Even the demons believe that — and shudder.

20 You foolish man, do you want evidence that faith without deeds is useless?

21 Was not our ancestor Abraham considered righteous for what he did when he offered his son Isaac on the altar?

22 You see that his faith and his actions were working together, and his faith was made complete by what he did.

23 And the scripture was fulfilled that says, "Abraham believed God, and it was credited to him as righteousness," and he was called God's friend.

OLD TESTAMENT

1 SAMUEL 17:36,37

36 [David said to King Saul,] Thy servant slew both the lion and the bear: and this uncircumcised Philistine shall be as one of them, seeing he hath defied the armies of the living God.

37 David said moreover, The Lord that delivered me out of the paw of the lion, and out of the

paw of the bear, he will deliver me out of the hand of this Philistine. And Saul said unto David, Go, and the Lord be with thee.

DANIEL 3:16-18

16 Shadrach, Meshach, and Abednego, answered and said to the king, O Nebuchadnezzar, we are not careful to answer thee in this matter.

17 If it be so [that you put us in the furnace], our God whom we serve is able to deliver us from the burning fiery furnace, and he will deliver us out of thine hand, O king.

18 But if not [if you don't put us in the furnace], be it known unto thee, O king, that we will not serve thy gods, nor worship the golden image which thou hast set up.

Overcomer's Confession:

I walk by faith and not by sight. By faith, I receive all the promises of God!

FAVOR

Friendly or kind regard; good will;
approval; liking.

NEW TESTAMENT

LUKE 2:52

52 And Jesus increased in wisdom and stature, and in favour with God and man.

ACTS 2:46,47

46 And they [the Early Church], continuing daily with one accord in the temple, and breaking bread from house to house, did eat their meat with gladness and singleness of heart,

47 Praising God, and having favour with all the people. And the Lord added to the church daily such as should be saved.

EPHESIANS 6:24 *(Amplified)*

24 Grace (God's undeserved favor) be with all who love our Lord Jesus Christ with undying and incorruptible [love]. Amen (so let it be).

2 PETER 1:2 *(Amplified)*

2 May grace (God's favor) and peace (which is perfect well-being, all necessary good, all spiritual prosperity, and freedom from fears and agitating

passions and moral conflicts) be multiplied to
you in [the full, personal, precise, and correct]
knowledge of God and of Jesus our Lord.

OLD TESTAMENT

PSALM 5:12
12 For thou, Lord, wilt bless the righteous; with
favour wilt thou compass him as with a shield.

PROVERBS 3:3,4 (*Amplified*)
3 Let not mercy and kindness [shutting out all
hatred and selfishness] and truth [shutting out
all deliberate hypocrisy or falsehood] forsake
you; bind them about your neck, write them
upon the tablet of your heart.
4 So shall you find favor, good understanding,
and high esteem in the sight [or judgment] of
God and man.

GENESIS 12:2 (*Amplified*)
2 And I will make of you [Abraham] a great
nation, and I will bless you [with abundant
increase of favors] and make your name
famous and distinguished, and you will be a
blessing [dispensing good to others].

GENESIS 39:21

21 But the Lord was with Joseph, and shewed him mercy, and gave him favour in the sight of the keeper of the prison.

DANIEL 1:9

9 Now God had brought Daniel into favour and tender love with the prince of the eunuchs.

Overcomer's Confession:

Father, I thank You that I have favor today. People are going out of their way to bless me and to do good to me today. Favor follows me everywhere I go!

FINANCES

The supplying and administration of money,
capital, vestments, and funds.

NEW TESTAMENT

LUKE 6:38

38 Give, and it shall be given unto you; good measure, pressed down, and shaken together, and running over, shall men give into your bosom. For with the same measure that ye mete withal it shall be measured to you again.

2 CORINTHIANS 9:6-8 (*Amplified*)

6 [Remember] this: he who sows sparingly and grudgingly will also reap sparingly and grudgingly, and he who sows generously [that blessings may come to someone] will also reap generously and with blessings.

7 Let each one [give] as he has made up his own mind and purposed in his heart, not reluctantly or sorrowfully or under compulsion, for God loves (He takes pleasure in, prizes above other things, and is unwilling to abandon or to do without) a cheerful (joyous, "prompt to do it") giver [whose heart is in his giving].

8 And God is able to make all grace (every favor and earthly blessing) come to you in abundance, so that you may always and under all

circumstances and whatever the need be self-sufficient [possessing enough to require no aid or support and furnished in abundance for every good work and charitable donation].

PHILIPPIANS 4:19

19 But my God shall supply all your need according to his riches in glory by Christ Jesus.

GALATIANS 3:13,14

13 Christ hath redeemed us from the curse of the law, being made a curse for us: for it is written, Cursed is every one that hangeth on a tree:

14 That the blessing of Abraham might come on the Gentiles through Jesus Christ; that we might receive the promise of the Spirit through faith.

OLD TESTAMENT

GENESIS 13:1,2

1 And Abram went up out of Egypt, he, and his wife, and all that he had, and Lot with him, into the south.

2 And Abram was very rich in cattle, in silver, and in gold.

DEUTERONOMY 28:1-8

1 And it shall come to pass, if thou shalt hearken diligently unto the voice of the Lord thy God, to

observe and to do all his commandments which I command thee this day, that the Lord thy God will set thee on high above all nations of the earth:

2 And all these blessings shall come on thee, and overtake thee, if thou shalt hearken unto the voice of the Lord thy God.

3 Blessed shalt thou be in the city, and blessed shalt thou be in the field.

4 Blessed shall be the fruit of thy body, and the fruit of thy ground, and the fruit of thy cattle, the increase of thy kine, and the flocks of thy sheep.

5 Blessed shall be thy basket and thy store.

6 Blessed shalt thou be when thou comest in, and blessed shalt thou be when thou goest out.

7 The Lord shall cause thine enemies that rise up against thee to be smitten before thy face: they shall come out against thee one way, and flee before thee seven ways.

8 The Lord shall command the blessing upon thee in thy storehouses, and in all that thou settest thine hand unto; and he shall bless thee in the land which the Lord thy God giveth thee.

MALACHI 3:10,11

10 Bring ye all the tithes into the storehouse, that there may be meat in mine house, and prove me now herewith, saith the Lord of hosts, if I will not open you the windows of heaven, and

pour you out a blessing, that there shall not be room enough to receive it.

11 And I will rebuke the devourer for your sakes, and he shall not destroy the fruits of your ground; neither shall your vine cast her fruit before the time in the field, saith the Lord of hosts.

Overcomer's Confession:

God is prospering me today. Because I have given, money cometh to me now. The angels are working, bringing my money in!

G

GOSSIP

Rumor or talk about others of a personal, sensational, or intimate nature.

NEW TESTAMENT

LUKE 6:45

45 A good man out of the good treasure of his heart bringeth forth that which is good; and an evil man out of the evil treasure of his heart bringeth forth that which is evil: for of the abundance of the heart his mouth speaketh.

1 TIMOTHY 5:13 *(NIV)*

13 Besides, they [the younger widows] get into the habit of being idle and going about from house to house. And not only do they become idlers, but also gossips and busybodies, saying things they ought not to.

TITUS 2:3 *(NIV)*

3 Likewise, teach the older women to be reverent in the way they live, not to be slanderers or addicted to much wine, but to teach what is good.

1 TIMOTHY 3:11 (*NIV*)

11 In the same way, their [the deacons'] wives are to be women worthy of respect, not malicious talkers but temperate and trustworthy in everything.

1 PETER 3:10

10 For he that will love life, and see good days, let him refrain his tongue from evil, and his lips that they speak no guile.

MATTHEW 12:36

36 But I say unto you, That every idle word that men shall speak, they shall give account thereof in the day of judgment.

OLD TESTAMENT

LEVITICUS 19:16 (*Amplified*)

16 You shall not go up and down as a dispenser of gossip and scandal among your people, nor shall you [secure yourself by false testimony or by silence and] endanger the life of your neighbor. I am the Lord.

PSALM 50:20

20 Thou sittest and speakest against thy brother; thou slanderest thine own mother's son.

PROVERBS 11:13

13 A talebearer revealeth secrets: but he that is of a faithful spirit concealeth the matter.

PROVERBS 20:19 (*NIV*)

19 A gossip betrays a confidence; so avoid a man who talks too much.

Overcomer's Confession:

Holy Spirit, put a watch over my mouth. Help me to speak only those things that are edifying to others.

GRACE

*The unmerited love and favor of God
toward man.*

NEW TESTAMENT

ROMANS 5:1,2

1   Therefore being justified by faith, we have
    peace with God through our Lord Jesus Christ:
2   By whom also we have access by faith into this
    grace wherein we stand, and rejoice in hope of
    the glory of God.

ROMANS 5:21

21 That as sin hath reigned unto death, even so
    might grace reign through righteousness unto
    eternal life by Jesus Christ our Lord.

1 CORINTHIANS 15:10

10 But by the grace of God I am what I am: and his
    grace which was bestowed upon me was not in
    vain; but I laboured more abundantly than they
    all: yet not I, but the grace of God which was
    with me.

EPHESIANS 4:7

7   But unto every one of us is given grace accord-
    ing to the measure of the gift of Christ.

2 CORINTHIANS 9:8

8 And God is able to make all grace abound toward you; that ye, always having all sufficiency in all things, may abound to every good work.

EPHESIANS 1:7,8 (*NIV*)

7 In him we have redemption through his blood, the forgiveness of sins, in accordance with the riches of God's grace

8 that he lavished on us with all wisdom and understanding.

EPHESIANS 2:8,9

8 For by grace are ye saved through faith; and that not of yourselves: it is the gift of God:

9 Not of works, lest any man should boast.

1 PETER 4:10 (*Amplified*)

10 As each of you has received a gift (a particular spiritual talent, a gracious divine endowment), employ it for one another as [befits] good trustees of God's many-sided grace [faithful stewards of the extremely diverse powers and gifts granted to Christians by unmerited favor].

TITUS 3:4-7

4 But after that the kindness and love of God our Saviour toward man appeared,

5   Not by works of righteousness which we have
    done, but according to his mercy he saved us,
    by the washing of regeneration, and renewing
    of the Holy Ghost;
6   Which he shed on us abundantly through Jesus
    Christ our Saviour;
7   That being justified by his grace, we should be
    made heirs according to the hope of eternal life

HEBREWS 4:16 (*Amplified*)

16 Let us then fearlessly and confidently and
    boldly draw near to the throne of grace (the
    throne of God's unmerited favor to us sinners),
    that we may receive mercy [for our failures]
    and find grace to help in good time for every
    need [appropriate help and well-timed help,
    coming just when we need it].

1 PETER 5:5

5   Likewise, ye younger, submit yourselves unto
    the elder. Yea, all of you be subject one to
    another, and be clothed with humility: for God
    resisteth the proud, and giveth grace to the
    humble.

OLD TESTAMENT

GENESIS 6:7,8

7   And the Lord said, I will destroy man whom I
    have created from the face of the earth; both

man, and beast, and the creeping thing, and the fowls of the air; for it repenteth me that I have made them.

8 But Noah found grace in the eyes of the Lord.

PSALM 84:11

11 For the Lord God is a sun and shield: the Lord will give grace and glory: no good thing will he withhold from them that walk uprightly.

PROVERBS 3:34

34 Surely he [God] scorneth the scorners: but he giveth grace unto the lowly.

Overcomer's Confession:

I use the gifts God has given me by His grace to bless others. And because of His gracious love, God withholds no good thing from me!

GREED

An excessive urge to attain more than what one needs or deserves, particularly in regard to material wealth.

NEW TESTAMENT

MATTHEW 6:19-21

19 Lay not up for yourselves treasures upon earth, where moth and rust doth corrupt, and where thieves break through and steal:

20 But lay up for yourselves treasures in heaven, where neither moth nor rust doth corrupt, and where thieves do not break through nor steal:

21 For where your treasure is, there will your heart be also.

MATTHEW 6:24 (*Amplified*)

24 No one can serve two masters; for either he will hate the one and love the other, or he will stand by and be devoted to the one and despise and be against the other. You cannot serve God and mammon (deceitful riches, money, possessions, or whatever is trusted in).

MATTHEW 6:31-33

31 Therefore take no thought, saying, What shall we eat? or, What shall we drink? or, Wherewithal shall we be clothed?

32 (For after all these things do the Gentiles seek:) for your heavenly Father knoweth that ye have need of all these things.

33 But seek ye first the kingdom of God, and his righteousness; and all these things shall be added unto you.

MATTHEW 13:22 (*Amplified*)

22 As for what was sown among thorns, this is he who hears the Word, but the cares of the world and the pleasure and delight and glamour and deceitfulness of riches choke and suffocate the Word, and it yields no fruit.

EPHESIANS 5:3 (*NIV*)

3 But among you there must not be even a hint of sexual immorality, or of any kind of impurity, or of greed, because these are improper for God's holy people.

COLOSSIANS 3:2

2 Set your affection on things above, not on things on the earth.

1 TIMOTHY 3:2,3 (*NIV*)

2 Now the overseer must be above reproach, the husband of but one wife, temperate, self-controlled, respectable, hospitable, able to teach,

3   not given to drunkenness, not violent but gentle, not quarrelsome, not a lover of money.

1 TIMOTHY 6:6
6   But godliness with contentment is great gain.

1 TIMOTHY 6:17
17   Charge them that are rich in this world, that they be not highminded, nor trust in uncertain riches, but in the living God, who giveth us richly all things to enjoy.

1 PETER 5:2 (*NIV*)
2   Be shepherds of God's flock that is under your care, serving as overseers — not because you must, but because you are willing, as God wants you to be; not greedy for money, but eager to serve.

OLD TESTAMENT

NEHEMIAH 5:7
7   Then I consulted with myself, and I rebuked the nobles, and the rulers, and said unto them, Ye exact usury, every one of his brother. And I set a great assembly against them.

PROVERBS 1:17-19 (*NIV*)

17 How useless to spread a net in full view of all the birds!
18 These men lie in wait for their own blood; they waylay only themselves!
19 Such is the end of all who go after ill-gotten gain; it takes away the lives of those who get it.

PROVERBS 11:24,25 (*NIV*)

24 One man gives freely, yet gains even more; another withholds unduly, but comes to poverty.
25 A generous man will prosper; he who refreshes others will himself be refreshed.

PROVERBS 15:27 (*Amplified*)

27 He who is greedy for unjust gain troubles his own household, but he who hates bribes will live.

ISAIAH 56:11

11 Yea, they are greedy dogs which can never have enough, and they are shepherds that cannot understand: they all look to their own way, every one for his gain, from his quarter.

EZEKIEL 22:12

12 In thee [Jerusalem] have they taken gifts to shed blood; thou hast taken usury and increase, and thou hast greedily gained of thy neighbours by extortion, and hast forgotten me, saith the Lord God.

HAGGAI 1:6,7

6 Ye have sown much, and bring in little; ye eat, but ye have not enough; ye drink, but ye are not filled with drink; ye clothe you, but there is none warm; and he that earneth wages earneth wages to put it into a bag with holes.

7 Thus saith the Lord of hosts; Consider your ways.

Overcomer's Confession:

I am not greedy of material gain. Instead, I am a generous giver. Thank You, Lord, that the fruit of the Spirit is working in me today.

GUILT

Being accountable for the commission
of a transgression; Repentant consciousness
or remorse for an offense.

NEW TESTAMENT

1 JOHN 3:19-21 (*Amplified*)

19 By this we shall come to know (perceive, recognize, and understand) that we are of the Truth, and can reassure (quiet, conciliate, and pacify) our hearts in His presence,

20 Whenever our hearts in [tormenting] self-accusation make us feel guilty and condemn us. [For we are in God's hands.] For He is above and greater than our consciences (our hearts), and He knows (perceives and understands) everything [nothing is hidden from Him].

21 And, beloved, if our consciences (our hearts) do not accuse us [if they do not make us feel guilty and condemn us], we have confidence [complete assurance and boldness] before God.

ACTS 2:36-38

36 Therefore let all the house of Israel know assuredly, that God hath made that same Jesus, whom ye have crucified, both Lord and Christ.

37 Now when they heard this, they were pricked in their heart, and said unto Peter and to the rest of the apostles, Men and brethren, what shall we do?

38 Then Peter said unto them, Repent, and be baptized every one of you in the name of Jesus Christ for the remission of sins, and ye shall receive the gift of the Holy Ghost.

ACTS 9:1-6

1 And Saul, yet breathing out threatenings and slaughter against the disciples of the Lord, went unto the high priest,

2 And desired of him letters to Damascus to the synagogues, that if he found any of this way, whether they were men or women, he might bring them bound unto Jerusalem.

3 And as he journeyed, he came near Damascus: and suddenly there shined round about him a light from heaven:

4 And he fell to the earth, and heard a voice saying unto him, Saul, Saul, why persecutest thou me?

5 And he said, Who art thou, Lord? And the Lord said, I am Jesus whom thou persecutest: it is hard for thee to kick against the pricks.

6 And he trembling and astonished said, Lord, what wilt thou have me to do? And the Lord said unto him, Arise, and go into the city, and it shall be told thee what thou must do.

MATTHEW 27:3

3 Then Judas, which had betrayed him, when he saw that he was condemned, repented himself, and brought again the thirty pieces of silver to the chief priests and elders.

LUKE 5:8

8 When Simon Peter saw it, he fell down at Jesus' knees, saying, Depart from me; for I am a sinful man, O Lord.

OLD TESTAMENT

ISAIAH 6:5-7

5 Then said I [the prophet Isaiah], Woe is me! for I am undone; because I am a man of unclean lips, and I dwell in the midst of a people of unclean lips: for mine eyes have seen the King, the Lord of hosts.
6 Then flew one of the seraphims unto me, having a live coal in his hand, which he had taken with the tongs from off the altar:
7 And he laid it upon my mouth, and said, Lo, this hath touched thy lips; and thine iniquity is taken away, and thy sin purged.

LAMENTATIONS 1:20 (NIV)

20 "See, O Lord, how distressed I am! I am in torment within, and in my heart I am disturbed,

for I have been most rebellious. Outside, the sword bereaves; inside, there is only death."

PSALMS 51:1,2 (*NIV*)

1 Have mercy on me, O God, according to your unfailing love; according to your great compassion blot out my transgressions.
2 Wash away all my iniquity and cleanse me from my sin.

Overcomer's Confession:

I will not feel guilty because my sins are washed away by the blood of Jesus. Thank You, Lord, for setting me free from guilt!

H

HATE

To feel malice or enmity toward; to despise.

NEW TESTAMENT

MATTHEW 10:22

22 And ye shall be hated of all men for my name's sake: but he that endureth to the end shall be saved.

LUKE 6:22,23

22 Blessed are ye, when men shall hate you, and when they shall separate you from their company, and shall reproach you, and cast out your name as evil, for the Son of man's sake.

23 Rejoice ye in that day, and leap for joy: for, behold, your reward is great in heaven: for in the like manner did their fathers unto the prophets.

LUKE 6:27,28

27 But I say unto you which hear, Love your enemies, do good to them which hate you,

28 Bless them that curse you, and pray for them which despitefully use you.

TITUS 3:3,4

3   For we ourselves also were sometimes foolish, disobedient, deceived, serving divers lusts and pleasures, living in malice and envy, hateful, and hating one another.

4   But after that the kindness and love of God our Saviour toward man appeared.

1 JOHN 2:9,10

9   He that saith he is in the light, and hateth his brother, is in darkness even until now.

10   He that loveth his brother abideth in the light, and there is none occasion of stumbling in him.

OLD TESTAMENT

GENESIS 37:5-8

5   And Joseph dreamed a dream, and he told it his brethren: and they hated him yet the more.

6   And he said unto them, Hear, I pray you, this dream which I have dreamed:

7   For, behold, we were binding sheaves in the field, and, lo, my sheaf arose, and also stood upright; and, behold, your sheaves stood round about, and made obeisance to my sheaf.

8   And his brethren said to him, Shalt thou indeed reign over us? or shalt thou indeed have dominion over us? And they hated him yet the more for his dreams, and for his words.

EXODUS 23:4,5 (*NIV*)

4 "If you come across your enemy's ox or donkey wandering off, be sure to take it back to him.

5 If you see the donkey of someone who hates you fallen down under its load, do not leave it there; be sure you help him with it."

LEVITICUS 19:17 (*NIV*)

17 "Do not hate your brother in your heart. Rebuke your neighbor frankly so you will not share in his guilt."

PSALM 9:13

13 Have mercy upon me, O Lord; consider my trouble which I suffer of them that hate me, thou that liftest me up from the gates of death.

PSALM 35:19

19 Let not them that are mine enemies wrongfully rejoice over me: neither let them wink with the eye that hate me without a cause.

PROVERBS 1:29-33

29 For that they hated knowledge, and did not choose the fear of the Lord:

30 They would none of my counsel: they despised all my reproof.

31 Therefore shall they eat of the fruit of their
    own way, and be filled with their own devices.
32 For the turning away of the simple shall slay
    them, and the prosperity of fools shall destroy
    them.
33 But whoso hearkeneth unto me shall dwell
    safely, and shall be quiet from fear of evil.

Overcomer's Confession:

I do not hate those who wrong me. I choose to forgive them, pray for them, and live a life of love.

HEALING

*To return to health or freedom from disease;
made well.*

NEW TESTAMENT

1 PETER 2:24

24 Who his [Jesus'] own self bare our sins in his
own body on the tree, that we, being dead to
sins, should live unto righteousness: by whose
stripes ye were healed.

MATTHEW 9:35

35 And Jesus went about all the cities and villages,
teaching in their synagogues, and preaching the
gospel of the kingdom, and healing every sickness and every disease among the people.

MATTHEW 10:1

1 And when he [Jesus] had called unto him his
twelve disciples, he gave them power against
unclean spirits, to cast them out, and to heal all
manner of sickness and all manner of disease.

MARK 16:17,18

17 And these signs shall follow them that believe;
In my name shall they cast out devils; they
shall speak with new tongues;

18 They shall take up serpents; and if they drink any deadly thing, it shall not hurt them; they shall lay hands on the sick, and they shall recover.

JAMES 5:14

14 Is any sick among you? let him call for the elders of the church; and let them pray over him, anointing him with oil in the name of the Lord.

ACTS 10:38

38 How God anointed Jesus of Nazareth with the Holy Ghost and with power: who went about doing good, and healing all that were oppressed of the devil; for God was with him.

OLD TESTAMENT

EXODUS 15:26

26 And [God] said, If thou wilt diligently hearken to the voice of the Lord thy God, and wilt do that which is right in his sight, and wilt give ear to his commandments, and keep all his statutes, I will put none of these diseases upon thee, which I have brought upon the Egyptians: for I am the Lord that healeth thee.

ISAIAH 53:4,5

4   Surely he hath borne our griefs, and carried
    our sorrows: yet we did esteem him stricken,
    smitten of God, and afflicted.
5   But he was wounded for our transgressions, he
    was bruised for our iniquities: the chastise-
    ment of our peace was upon him; and with his
    stripes we are healed.

JEREMIAH 17:14

14 Heal me, O Lord, and I shall be healed; save me,
    and I shall be saved: for thou art my praise.

Overcomer's Confession:

I am healed by the stripes of Jesus. I walk in
divine health. Every sickness, disease, virus, or
germ that touches my body dies instantly in the
Name of Jesus!

HUSBANDS (*see* WIFE)

A man with reference to the woman
to whom he is married.

NEW TESTAMENT

EPHESIANS 5:25-28

25 Husbands, love your wives, even as Christ also loved the church, and gave himself for it;
26 That he might sanctify and cleanse it with the washing of water by the word,
27 That he might present it to himself a glorious church, not having spot, or wrinkle, or any such thing; but that it should be holy and without blemish.
28 So ought men to love their wives as their own bodies. He that loveth his wife loveth himself.

1 PETER 3:7 (*NIV*)

7 Husbands, in the same way be considerate as you live with your wives, and treat them with respect as the weaker partner and as heirs with you of the gracious gift of life, so that nothing will hinder your prayers.

COLOSSIANS 3:19 (*Amplified*)

19 Husbands, love your wives [be affectionate and sympathetic with them] and do not be harsh or bitter or resentful toward them.

OLD TESTAMENT

PROVERBS 5:15-19

15 Drink waters out of thine own cistern, and running waters out of thine own well.

16 Let thy fountains be dispersed abroad, and rivers of waters in the streets.

17 Let them be only thine own, and not strangers' with thee.

18 Let thy fountain be blessed: and rejoice with the wife of thy youth.

19 Let her be as the loving hind and pleasant roe; let her breasts satisfy thee at all times; and be thou ravished always with her love.

PROVERBS 31:23,28

23 Her [the virtuous woman's] husband is known in the gates, when he sitteth among the elders of the land . . . .

28 Her children arise up, and call her blessed; her husband also, and he praiseth her.

MALACHI 2:13-15 (NIV)

13 Another thing you do: You flood the Lord's altar with tears. You weep and wail because he no longer pays attention to your offerings or accepts them with pleasure from your hands.

14 You ask, "Why?" It is because the Lord is acting as the witness between you and the wife of your youth, because you have broken faith with

her, though she is your partner, the wife of your marriage covenant.

15 Has not [the Lord] made them one? In flesh and spirit they are his. And why one? Because he was seeking godly offspring. So guard yourself in your spirit, and do not break faith with the wife of your youth.

Overcomer's Confession:

[Men:] I love my wife as Christ loves the Church. My prayers are unhindered because I treat her with respect and consideration as a fellow heir of the grace of life.

[Women:] My husband loves me as Christ loves the Church. He treats me with respect and consideration as a fellow heir of the grace of life.

I

INCREASE

To become bigger or greater; to enlarge; multiply.

NEW TESTAMENT

LUKE 6:38 (*Amplified*)

38 Give, and [gifts] will be given to you; good measure, pressed down, shaken together, and running over, will they pour into [the pouch formed by] the bosom [of your robe and used as a bag]. For with the measure you deal out [with the measure you use when you confer benefits on others], it will be measured back to you.

1 CORINTHIANS 3:6,7

6 I have planted, Apollos watered; but God gave the increase.

7 So then neither is he that planteth any thing, neither he that watereth; but God that giveth the increase.

2 CORINTHIANS 9:10,11 (*NIV*)

10 Now he who supplies seed to the sower and bread for food will also supply and increase

your store of seed and will enlarge the harvest
of your righteousness.

11 You will be made rich in every way so that you
can be generous on every occasion, and through
us your generosity will result in thanksgiving
to God.

1 THESSALONIANS 3:12

12 And the Lord make you to increase and abound
in love one toward another, and toward all
men, even as we do toward you.

1 THESSALONIANS 4:9,10

9   But as touching brotherly love ye need not that
I write unto you: for ye yourselves are taught of
God to love one another.

10 And indeed ye do it toward all the brethren
which are in all Macedonia: but we beseech
you, brethren, that ye increase more and more.

OLD TESTAMENT

DEUTERONOMY 6:3

3   Hear therefore, O Israel, and observe to do it;
that it may be well with thee, and that ye may
increase mightily, as the Lord God of thy
fathers hath promised thee, in the land that
floweth with milk and honey.

PSALM 71:21

21 Thou shalt increase my greatness, and comfort me on every side.

PSALM 115:13,14

13 He will bless them that fear the Lord, both small and great.

14 The Lord shall increase you more and more, you and your children.

PROVERBS 1:5

5 A wise man will hear, and will increase learning; and a man of understanding shall attain unto wise counsels.

ISAIAH 29:19

19 The meek also shall increase their joy in the Lord, and the poor among men shall rejoice in the Holy One of Israel.

Overcomer's Confession:

The Lord is increasing me more and more. I am increasing in favor, money, wisdom, love — in every area of my life. Thank You, Lord, for bringing me increase!

INTEGRITY

*Unwavering adherence to sound moral principles
of uprightness, honesty, and sincerity.*

NEW TESTAMENT

2 CORINTHIANS 4:1,2

1   Therefore seeing we have this ministry, as we have received mercy, we faint not;
2   But have renounced the hidden things of dishonesty, not walking in craftiness, nor handling the word of God deceitfully; but by manifestation of the truth commending ourselves to every man's conscience in the sight of God.

LUKE 16:10 (*NIV*)

10 "Whoever can be trusted with very little can also be trusted with much, and whoever is dishonest with very little will also be dishonest with much."

ACTS 23:1

1   And Paul, earnestly beholding the council, said, Men and brethren, I have lived in all good conscience before God until this day.

ACTS 24:16 (*Amplified*)

16 Therefore I always exercise and discipline myself [mortifying my body, deadening my carnal affections, bodily appetites, and worldly desires, endeavoring in all respects] to have a clear (unshaken, blameless) conscience, void of offense toward God and toward men.

2 CORINTHIANS 7:2

2 Receive us; we have wronged no man, we have corrupted no man, we have defrauded no man.

2 CORINTHIANS 8:21 (*NIV*)

21 For we are taking pains to do what is right, not only in the eyes of the Lord but also in the eyes of men.

PHILIPPIANS 4:8

8 Finally, brethren, whatsoever things are true, whatsoever things are honest, whatsoever things are just, whatsoever things are pure, whatsoever things are lovely, whatsoever things are of good report; if there be any virtue, and if there be any praise, think on these things.

EPHESIANS 6:5,6 (*NIV*)

5   Slaves, obey your earthly masters with respect and fear, and with sincerity of heart, just as you would obey Christ.

6   Obey them not only to win their favor when their eye is on you, but like slaves of Christ, doing the will of God from your heart.

OLD TESTAMENT

PSALM 7:10

10 My defence is of God, which saveth the upright in heart.

PROVERBS 10:29

29 The way of the Lord is strength to the upright: but destruction shall be to the workers of iniquity.

PROVERBS 11:3

3   The integrity of the upright shall guide them: but the perverseness of transgressors shall destroy them.

Overcomer's Confession:

I walk uprightly before the Lord and do those things that are pleasing to Him. Thank You, Lord, for helping me glorify You today.

J

JEALOUSY

Embittered or resentful in rivalry; covetous.

NEW TESTAMENT

ROMANS 13:13,14 (*NIV*)

13 Let us behave decently, as in the daytime, not in orgies and drunkenness, not in sexual immorality and debauchery, not in dissension and jealousy.

14 Rather, clothe yourselves with the Lord Jesus Christ, and do not think about how to gratify the desires of the sinful nature.

1 CORINTHIANS 3:3

3 For ye are yet carnal: for whereas there is among you envying, and strife, and divisions, are ye not carnal, and walk as men?

GALATIANS 5:26

26 Let us not be desirous of vain glory, provoking one another, envying one another.

JAMES 3:14-16 (*Amplified*)

14 But if you have bitter jealousy (envy) and contention (rivalry, selfish ambition) in your

hearts, do not pride yourselves on it and thus be in defiance of and false to the Truth.

15 This [superficial] wisdom is not such as comes down from above, but is earthly, unspiritual (animal), even devilish (demoniacal).

16 For wherever there is jealousy (envy) and contention (rivalry and selfish ambition), there will also be confusion (unrest, disharmony, rebellion) and all sorts of evil and vile practices.

ACTS 13:45 (*NIV*)

45 When the Jews saw the crowds, they were filled with jealousy and talked abusively against what Paul was saying.

OLD TESTAMENT

PROVERBS 6:34

34 For jealousy is the rage of a man: therefore he will not spare in the day of vengeance.

PROVERBS 27:4

4 Wrath is cruel, and anger is outrageous; but who is able to stand before envy?

ECCLESIASTES 4:4 (NIV)

4 And I saw that all labor and all achievement spring from man's envy of his neighbor. This too is meaningless, a chasing after the wind.

SONG OF SOLOMON 8:6

6 Set me as a seal upon thine heart, as a seal upon thine arm: for love is strong as death; jealousy is cruel as the grave: the coals thereof are coals of fire, which hath a most vehement flame.

Overcomer's Confession:

I am not jealous because I walk in love. God's love in me is greater then the feelings of jealousy. I will resist the temptation to be jealous. Thank You, Lord, for setting me free!

JOY

Profound and jubilant cheer; happiness; delight.

NEW TESTAMENT

JAMES 1:2,3 *(Amplified)*

2 Consider it wholly joyful, my brethren, whenever you are enveloped in or encounter trials of
any sort or fall into various temptations.

3 Be assured and understand that the trial and
proving of your faith bring out endurance and
steadfastness and patience.

MATTHEW 25:21

21 His lord said unto him [the man with five talents who gained another five], Well done, thou
good and faithful servant: thou hast been
faithful over a few things, I will make thee
ruler over many things: enter thou into the joy
of thy lord.

LUKE 15:10

10 Likewise, I say unto you, there is joy in the
presence of the angels of God over one sinner
that repenteth.

JOHN 15:10,11

10 If ye keep my commandments, ye shall abide in
my love; even as I have kept my Father's commandments, and abide in his love.

11 These things have I spoken unto you, that my
joy might remain in you, and that your joy
might be full.

JOHN 16:24

24 Hitherto have ye asked nothing in my name:
ask, and ye shall receive, that your joy may be
full.

ROMANS 14:17

17 For the kingdom of God is not meat and drink;
but righteousness, and peace, and joy in the
Holy Ghost.

ROMANS 15:13

13 Now the God of hope fill you with all joy and
peace in believing, that ye may abound in hope,
through the power of the Holy Ghost.

HEBREWS 12:2

2 Looking unto Jesus the author and finisher of
our faith; who for the joy that was set before
him endured the cross, despising the shame,

and is set down at the right hand of the throne of God.

HEBREWS 13:17

17 Obey them that have the rule over you, and submit yourselves: for they watch for your souls, as they that must give account, that they may do it with joy, and not with grief. for that is unprofitable for you.

1 PETER 1:8 (*Amplified*)

8 Without having seen Him [Jesus], you love Him; though you do not [even] now see Him, you believe in Him and exult and thrill with inexpressible and glorious (triumphant, heavenly) joy.

1 JOHN 1:4

4 And these things write we unto you, that your joy may be full.

JUDE 1:24 (*Amplified*)

24 Now to Him Who is able to keep you without stumbling or slipping or falling, and to present [you] unblemished (blameless and faultless) before the presence of His glory in triumphant joy and exultation [with unspeakable, ecstatic delight].

OLD TESTAMENT

1 KINGS 1:39,40

39 And Zadok the priest took an horn of oil out of the tabernacle, and anointed Solomon. And they blew the trumpet; and all the people said, God save king Solomon.

40 And all the people came up after him, and the people piped with pipes, and rejoiced with great joy, so that the earth rent with the sound of them.

1 CHRONICLES 15:16

16 And David spake to the chief of the Levites to appoint their brethren to be the singers with instruments of musick, psalteries and harps and cymbals, sounding, by lifting up the voice with joy.

NEHEMIAH 8:10

10 Then he [Ezra] said unto them [the Jewish people], Go your way, eat the fat, and drink the sweet, and send portions unto them for whom nothing is prepared: for this day is holy unto our Lord: neither be ye sorry; for the joy of the Lord is your strength.

PSALM 4:7

7   Thou hast put gladness in my heart, more than in the time that their corn and their wine increased.

PSALM 16:11

11 Thou wilt shew me the path of life: in thy presence is fulness of joy; at thy right hand there are pleasures for evermore.

PSALM 21:6

6   For thou hast made him [King David] most blessed for ever: thou hast made him exceeding glad with thy countenance.

Overcomer's Confession:

The joy of the Lord is my strength. I will not let anything steal my joy today!

K

KINDNESS

*The quality of being friendly, generous,
sympathetic, tenderhearted, and
affectionate to others.*

NEW TESTAMENT

EPHESIANS 4:32

32 And be ye kind one to another, tenderhearted,
forgiving one another, even as God for Christ's
sake hath forgiven you.

MATTHEW 5:7

7 Blessed are the merciful: for they shall obtain
mercy.

MATTHEW 5:42

42 Give to him that asketh thee, and from him
that would borrow of thee turn not thou away.

LUKE 6:33 (*NIV*)

33 "And if you do good to those who are good to
you, what credit is that to you? Even 'sinners'
do that."

Romans 15:1,2 (*Amplified*)

1   We who are strong [in our convictions and of robust faith] ought to bear with the failings and the frailties and the tender scruples of the weak; [we ought to help carry the doubts and qualms of others] and not to please ourselves.
2   Let each one of us make it a practice to please (make happy) his neighbor for his good and for his true welfare, to edify him [to strengthen him and build him up spiritually].

Galatians 6:1

1   Brethren, if a man be overtaken in a fault, ye which are spiritual, restore such an one in the spirit of meekness; considering thyself, lest thou also be tempted.

Galatians 6:10 (*Amplified*)

10   So then, as occasion and opportunity open up to us, let us do good [morally] to all people [not only being useful or profitable to them, but also doing what is for their spiritual good and advantage]. Be mindful to be a blessing, especially to those of the household of faith [those who belong to God's family with you, the believers].

OLD TESTAMENT

LEVITICUS 19:34

34 But the stranger that dwelleth with you shall be unto you as one born among you, and thou shalt love him as thyself; for ye were strangers in the land of Egypt: I am the Lord your God.

PSALM 112:5

5 A good man sheweth favour, and lendeth: he will guide his affairs with discretion.

PROVERBS 31:26

26 She [the virtuous woman] openeth her mouth with wisdom; and in her tongue is the law of kindness.

ZECHARIAH 7:9

9 Thus speaketh the Lord of hosts, saying, Execute true judgment, and shew mercy and compassions every man to his brother.

Overcomer's Confession:

I am reaching out in love with words and deeds of kindness. Thank You, Lord, for making me a witness of Your love today.

KNOWLEDGE

Understanding, familiarity, or discernment of facts obtained by experiences or study.

NEW TESTAMENT

JOHN 8:32

32 And ye shall know the truth, and the truth shall make you free.

JOHN 7:17

17 If any man will do his [God's] will, he shall know of the doctrine, whether it be of God, or whether I speak of myself.

PHILIPPIANS 3:8

8 Yea doubtless, and I count all things but loss for the excellency of the knowledge of Christ Jesus my Lord: for whom I have suffered the loss of all things, and do count them but dung, that I may win Christ.

1 CORINTHIANS 13:9 *(Amplified)*

9 For our knowledge is fragmentary (incomplete and imperfect), and our prophecy (our teaching) is fragmentary (incomplete and imperfect).

ROMANS 15:14

14 And I myself also am persuaded of you, my brethren, that ye also are full of goodness, filled with all knowledge, able also to admonish one another.

2 CORINTHIANS 2:11

11 Lest Satan should get an advantage of us: for we are not ignorant of his devices.

COLOSSIANS 3:16

16 Let the word of Christ dwell in you richly in all wisdom; teaching and admonishing one another in psalms and hymns and spiritual songs, singing with grace in your hearts to the Lord.

1 TIMOTHY 2:3,4

3 For this is good and acceptable in the sight of God our Saviour;
4 Who will have all men to be saved, and to come unto the knowledge of the truth.

1 JOHN 4:7,8

7 Beloved, let us love one another: for love is of God; and every one that loveth is born of God, and knoweth God.
8 He that loveth not knoweth not God; for God is love.

OLD TESTAMENT

HOSEA 4:6

6   My people are destroyed for lack of knowledge: because thou hast rejected knowledge, I will also reject thee, that thou shalt be no priest to me: seeing thou hast forgotten the law of thy God, I will also forget thy children.

PROVERBS 24:5

5   A wise man is strong; yea, a man of knowledge increaseth strength.

1 KINGS 3:9

9   Give therefore thy servant an understanding heart to judge thy people, that I may discern between good and bad: for who is able to judge this thy so great a people?

PSALM 119:66

66 Teach me good judgment and knowledge: for I have believed thy commandments.

PROVERBS 12:1

1   Whoso loveth instruction loveth knowledge: but he that hateth reproof is brutish.

PROVERBS 15:14

14 The heart of him that hath understanding seeketh knowledge: but the mouth of fools feedeth on foolishness.

PROVERBS 18:15

15 The heart of the prudent getteth knowledge; and the ear of the wise seeketh knowledge.

Overcomer's Confession:

I am increasing in the knowledge of Jesus. The Holy Spirit is my Teacher.

L

LABOR

*Strenuous physical or intellectual
activity; work.*

NEW TESTAMENT

ACTS 20:35

35 I [Paul] have shewed you all things, how that so
labouring ye ought to support the weak, and to
remember the words of the Lord Jesus, how he
said, It is more blessed to give than to receive.

1 CORINTHIANS 9:9,10 (*NIV*)

9 For it is written in the Law of Moses: "Do not
muzzle an ox while it is treading out the
grain." Is it about oxen that God is concerned?
10 Surely he says this for us, doesn't he? Yes, this
was written for us, because when the plowman
plows and the thresher threshes, they ought to
do so in the hope of sharing in the harvest.

EPHESIANS 4:28

28 Let him that stole steal no more: but rather let
him labour, working with his hands the thing
which is good, that he may have to give to him
that needeth.

COLOSSIANS 3:23

23 And whatsoever ye do, do it heartily, as to the Lord, and not unto men.

1 THESSALONIANS 4:11

11 And that ye study to be quiet, and to do your own business, and to work with your own hands, as we commanded you.

2 THESSALONIANS 3:7-13

7   For yourselves know how ye ought to follow us: for we behaved not ourselves disorderly among you;

8   Neither did we eat any man's bread for nought; but wrought with labour and travail night and day, that we might not be chargeable to any of you:

9   Not because we have not power, but to make ourselves an ensample unto you to follow us.

10 For even when we were with you, this we commanded you, that if any would not work, neither should he eat.

11 For we hear that there are some which walk among you disorderly, working not at all, but are busybodies.

12 Now them that are such we command and exhort by our Lord Jesus Christ, that with quietness they work, and eat their own bread.

13 But ye, brethren, be not weary in well doing.

OLD TESTAMENT

GENESIS 3:19

19 In the sweat of thy face shalt thou eat bread, till thou return unto the ground; for out of it wast thou taken: for dust thou art, and unto dust shalt thou return.

LEVITICUS 19:13

13 Thou shalt not defraud thy neighbour, neither rob him: the wages of him that is hired shall not abide with thee all night until the morning.

DEUTERONOMY 24:14,15

14 Thou shalt not oppress an hired servant that is poor and needy, whether he be of thy brethren, or of thy strangers that are in thy land within thy gates:

15 At his day thou shalt give him his hire, neither shall the sun go down upon it; for he is poor, and setteth his heart upon it: lest he cry against thee unto the Lord, and it be sin unto thee.

DEUTERONOMY 28:8

8 The Lord shall command the blessing upon thee in thy storehouses, and in all that thou settest thine hand unto; and he shall bless thee in the land which the Lord thy God giveth thee.

ECCLESIASTES 5:12

12 The sleep of a labouring man is sweet, whether he eat little or much: but the abundance of the rich will not suffer him to sleep.

Overcomer's Confession:

As I do the work God has set before me, He blesses me with abundance in return. He prospers everything I put my hand to!

LAZINESS

*Rebellious against labor or activity;
inclined to inactivity or idleness.*

NEW TESTAMENT

HEBREWS 6:12 (*NIV*)

12 We do not want you to become lazy, but to imitate those who through faith and patience inherit what has been promised.

MATTHEW 25:26-28

26 His lord answered and said unto him [the servant who hid his one talent], Thou wicked and slothful servant, thou knewest that I reap where I sowed not, and gather where I have not strawed:

27 Thou oughtest therefore to have put my money to the exchangers, and then at my coming I should have received mine own with usury.

28 Take therefore the talent from him, and give it unto him which hath ten talents.

ROMANS 12:10,11

10 Be kindly affectioned one to another with brotherly love; in honour preferring one another;

11 Not slothful in business; fervent in spirit; serving the Lord.

2 THESSALONIANS 3:10,11

10 For even when we were with you, this we commanded you, that if any would not work, neither should he eat.
11 For we hear that there are some which walk
among you disorderly, working not at all, but
are busybodies.

MATTHEW 20:6,7

6 And about the eleventh hour he went out, and
found others standing idle, and saith unto
them, Why stand ye here all the day idle?
7 They say unto him, Because no man hath hired
us. He saith unto them, Go ye also into the
vineyard; and whatsoever is right, that shall ye
receive.

1 TIMOTHY 5:13

13 And withal they [the younger widows] learn to
be idle, wandering about from house to house;
and not only idle, but tattlers also and busybodies, speaking things which they ought not.

OLD TESTAMENT

PROVERBS 6:6-11

6 Go to the ant, thou sluggard; consider her ways,
and be wise:
7 Which having no guide, overseer, or ruler,

8 Provideth her meat in the summer, and gathereth her food in the harvest.
9 How long wilt thou sleep, O sluggard? when wilt thou arise out of thy sleep?
10 Yet a little sleep, a little slumber, a little folding of the hands to sleep:
11 So shall thy poverty come as one that travelleth, and thy want as an armed man.

PROVERBS 10:4,5

4 He becometh poor that dealeth with a slack hand: but the hand of the diligent maketh rich.
5 He that gathereth in summer is a wise son: but he that sleepeth in harvest is a son that causeth shame.

ECCLESIASTES 10:18

18 By much slothfulness the building decayeth; and through idleness of the hands the house droppeth through.

Overcomer's Confession:

I will not be lazy but will work diligently as unto the Lord. I will be a follower of those who by faith and patience inherit God's promises!

M

MARRIAGE

*The lawful joining of a man and woman
as husband and wife.*

NEW TESTAMENT

HEBREWS 13:4 (*Amplified*)

4 Let marriage be held in honor (esteemed worthy, precious, of great price, and especially dear) in all things. And thus let the marriage bed be undefiled (kept undishonored); for God will judge and punish the unchaste [all guilty of sexual vice] and adulterous.

MATTHEW 5:31,32

31 It hath been said, Whosoever shall put away his wife, let him give her a writing of divorcement:

32 But I say unto you, That whosoever shall put away his wife, saving for the cause of fornication, causeth her to commit adultery: and whosoever shall marry her that is divorced committeth adultery.

Romans 7:1-3

1 Know ye not, brethren, (for I speak to them that know the law,) how that the law hath dominion over a man as long as he liveth?

2 For the woman which hath an husband is bound by the law to her husband so long as he liveth; but if the husband be dead, she is loosed from the law of her husband.

3 So then if, while her husband liveth, she be married to another man, she shall be called an adulteress: but if her husband be dead, she is free from that law; so that she is no adulteress, though she be married to another man.

1 Corinthians 7:3-5 (*NIV*)

3 The husband should fulfill his marital duty to his wife, and likewise the wife to her husband.

4 The wife's body does not belong to her alone but also to her husband. In the same way, the husband's body does not belong to him alone but also to his wife.

5 Do not deprive each other except by mutual consent and for a time, so that you may devote yourselves to prayer. Then come together again so that Satan will not tempt you because of your lack of self-control.

1 Corinthians 11:11,12 (*Amplified*)

11 Nevertheless, in [the plan of] the Lord and from His point of view woman is not apart from and

independent of man, nor is man aloof from and independent of woman;

12 For as woman was made from man, even so man is also born of woman; and all [whether male or female go forth] from God [as their Author].

EPHESIANS 5:22,25

22 Wives, submit yourselves unto your own husbands, as unto the Lord. . . .

25 Husbands, love your wives, even as Christ also loved the church, and gave himself for it.

COLOSSIANS 3:18,19

18 Wives, submit yourselves unto your own husbands, as it is fit in the Lord.

19 Husbands, love your wives, and be not bitter against them.

1 TIMOTHY 5:14

14 I will therefore that the younger women marry, bear children, guide the house, give none occasion to the adversary to speak reproachfully.

1 PETER 3:1,2,7 (*NIV*)

1 Wives, in the same way be submissive to your husbands so that, if any of them do not believe the word, they may be won over without words by the behavior of their wives,

2   when they see the purity and reverence of your lives . . . .

7   Husbands, in the same way be considerate as you live with your wives, and treat them with respect as the weaker partner and as heirs with you of the gracious gift of life, so that nothing will hinder your prayers.

OLD TESTAMENT

GENESIS 2:23,24

23   And Adam said, This is now bone of my bones, and flesh of my flesh: she shall be called Woman, because she was taken out of Man.

24   Therefore shall a man leave his father and his mother, and shall cleave unto his wife: and they shall be one flesh.

PROVERBS 18:22

22   Whoso findeth a wife findeth a good thing, and obtaineth favour of the Lord.

Overcomer's Confession:

God is blessing my marriage. I walk in love toward my spouse. I prefer my spouse before myself because the love of God inside me never fails.

MERCY

Kindness and compassion in excess of what may be expected or demanded by fairness.

NEW TESTAMENT

LUKE 6:36

36 Be ye therefore merciful, as your Father also is merciful.

ROMANS 12:6,8

6 Having then gifts differing according to the grace that is given to us, whether prophecy, let us prophesy according to the proportion of faith. . . .

8 Or he that exhorteth, on exhortation: he that giveth, let him do it with simplicity; he that ruleth, with diligence; he that sheweth mercy, with cheerfulness.

JAMES 2:12,13 (*NIV*)

12 Speak and act as those who are going to be judged by the law that gives freedom,

13 because judgment without mercy will be shown to anyone who has not been merciful. Mercy triumphs over judgment!

MATTHEW 6:14,15

14 For if ye forgive men their trespasses, your heavenly Father will also forgive you:

15 But if ye forgive not men their trespasses, neither will your Father forgive your trespasses.

ROMANS 11:32 (*Amplified*)

32 For God has consigned (penned up) all men to disobedience, only that He may have mercy on them all [alike].

2 CORINTHIANS 1:3

3 Blessed be God, even the Father of our Lord Jesus Christ, the Father of mercies, and the God of all comfort.

1 TIMOTHY 1:12,13

12 And I thank Christ Jesus our Lord, who hath enabled me, for that he counted me faithful, putting me into the ministry;

13 Who was before a blasphemer, and a persecutor, and injurious: but I obtained mercy, because I did it ignorantly in unbelief.

OLD TESTAMENT

EXODUS 2:24,25 (*Amplified*)

24 And God heard their sighing and groaning and [earnestly] remembered His covenant with Abraham, with Isaac, and with Jacob.

25 God saw the Israelites and took knowledge of them and concerned Himself about them [knowing all, understanding, remembering all].

NUMBERS 14:18

18 The Lord is longsuffering, and of great mercy, forgiving iniquity and transgression, and by no means clearing the guilty, visiting the iniquity of the fathers upon the children unto the third and fourth generation.

DEUTERONOMY 4:31

31 (For the Lord thy God is a merciful God;) he will not forsake thee, neither destroy thee, nor forget the covenant of thy fathers which he sware unto them.

PSALM 31:7

7 I will be glad and rejoice in thy mercy: for thou hast considered my trouble; thou hast known my soul in adversities.

PSALM 32:1

1 Blessed is he whose transgression is forgiven, whose sin is covered.

PSALM 86:15

15 But thou, O Lord, art a God full of compassion, and gracious, longsuffering, and plenteous in mercy and truth.

Overcomer's Confession:

Thank You, Lord, for Your mercy. Because You are merciful to me, I will show mercy to others.

N

NEEDS

*Something that is useful, required,
or desired but is lacking.*

NEW TESTAMENT

PHILIPPIANS 4:19

19 But my God shall supply all your need according to his riches in glory by Christ Jesus.

MATTHEW 6:7,8

7 But when ye pray, use not vain repetitions, as the heathen do: for they think that they shall be heard for their much speaking.

8 Be not ye therefore like unto them: for your Father knoweth what things ye have need of, before ye ask him.

LUKE 9:11

11 And the people, when they knew it, followed him [Jesus]: and he received them, and spake unto them of the kingdom of God, and healed them that had need of healing.

ROMANS 12:13 (*NIV*)

13 Share with God's people who are in need. Practice hospitality.

1 CORINTHIANS 12:20-22

20 But now are they many members, yet but one body.

21 And the eye cannot say unto the hand, I have no need of thee: nor again the head to the feet, I have no need of you.

22 Nay, much more those members of the body, which seem to be more feeble, are necessary.

EPHESIANS 4:28 (*NIV*)

28 He who has been stealing must steal no longer, but must work, doing something useful with his own hands, that he may have something to share with those in need.

OLD TESTAMENT

DEUTERONOMY 15:7,8

7 If there be among you a poor man of one of thy brethren within any of thy gates in thy land which the Lord thy God giveth thee, thou shalt not harden thine heart, nor shut thine hand from thy poor brother:

8 But thou shalt open thine hand wide unto him, and shalt surely lend him sufficient for his need, in that which he wanteth.

Isaiah 58:10,11 (*NIV*)

10 And if you spend yourselves in behalf of the hungry and satisfy the needs of the oppressed, then your light will rise in the darkness, and your night will become like the noonday.

11 The Lord will guide you always; he will satisfy your needs in a sun-scorched land and will strengthen your frame. You will be like a well-watered garden, like a spring whose waters never fail.

Overcomer's Confession:

I will be sensitive to the needs of others. Thank You, Lord, for meeting all of my needs.

NEGLECT

To fail to attend to appropriately;
chronic insufficiency of responsibility.

NEW TESTAMENT

1 TIMOTHY 4:14,15 (*NIV*)

14 Do not neglect your gift, which was given you through a prophetic message when the body of elders laid their hands on you.

15 Be diligent in these matters; give yourself wholly to them, so that everyone may see your progress.

2 TIMOTHY 1:6

6 Wherefore I put thee in remembrance that thou stir up the gift of God, which is in thee by the putting on of my hands.

MATTHEW 18:15-17

15 Moreover if thy brother shall trespass against thee, go and tell him his fault between thee and him alone: if he shall hear thee, thou hast gained thy brother.

16 But if he will not hear thee, then take with thee one or two more, that in the mouth of two or three witnesses every word may be established.

17 And if he shall neglect to hear them, tell it unto
the church: but if he neglect to hear the church,
let him be unto thee as an heathen man and a
publican.

HEBREWS 2:3

3 How shall we escape, if we neglect so great salvation; which at the first began to be spoken by
the Lord, and was confirmed unto us by them
that heard him.

ACTS 6:1

1 And in those days, when the number of the disciples was multiplied, there arose a murmuring of
the Grecians against the Hebrews, because their
widows were neglected in the daily ministration.

OLD TESTAMENT

JOSHUA 18:3 (*Amplified*)

3 Joshua asked the Israelites, How long will you
be slack to go in and possess the land which
the Lord, the God of your fathers, has given
you?

NEHEMIAH 10:39 (*NIV*)

39 The people of Israel, including the Levites, are
to bring their contributions of grain, new wine
and oil to the storerooms where the articles for

the sanctuary are kept and where the ministering priests, the gatekeepers and the singers stay. "We will not neglect the house of our God."

Overcomer's Confession:

I will not neglect those things that are most important in my life, such as the Word of God, my spouse and children, or going to church. I will give myself wholly to the things of God, and my progress will be evident to all!

O

OBEDIENCE

The state of submitting to the control of or carrying out the instructions of another.

NEW TESTAMENT

LUKE 11:28 (*Amplified*)

28 But He said, Blessed (happy and to be envied) rather are those who hear the Word of God and obey and practice it!

MATTHEW 12:50

50 For whosoever shall do the will of my Father which is in heaven, the same is my brother, and sister, and mother.

JOHN 14:15

15 If ye love me, keep my commandments.

ACTS 4:19 (*NIV*)

19 But Peter and John replied, "Judge for yourselves whether it is right in God's sight to obey you rather than God."

ROMANS 6:17 (*Amplified*)

17 But thank God, though you were once slaves of sin, you have become obedient with all your heart to the standard of teaching in which you were instructed and to which you were committed.

HEBREWS 5:8

8 Though he were a Son, yet learned he obedience by the things which he suffered;

JAMES 1:22-25

22 But be ye doers of the word, and not hearers only, deceiving your own selves.

23 For if any be a hearer of the word, and not a doer, he is like unto a man beholding his natural face in a glass:

24 For he beholdeth himself, and goeth his way, and straightway forgetteth what manner of man he was.

25 But whoso looketh into the perfect law of liberty, and continueth therein, he being not a forgetful hearer, but a doer of the work, this man shall be blessed in his deed.

OLD TESTAMENT

GENESIS 18:19

19 For I know him [Abraham], that he will command his children and his household after him, and

they shall keep the way of the Lord, to do justice and judgment; that the Lord may bring upon Abraham that which he hath spoken of him.

EXODUS 24:7

7 And he [Moses] took the book of the covenant, and read in the audience of the people: and they said, All that the Lord hath said will we do, and be obedient.

NUMBERS 14:24

24 But my servant Caleb, because he had another spirit with him, and hath followed me fully, him will I bring into the land whereinto he went; and his seed shall possess it.

1 KINGS 3:14

14 And if thou wilt walk in my ways, to keep my statutes and my commandments, as thy father David did walk, then I will lengthen thy days.

JOSHUA 1:8

8 This book of the law shall not depart out of thy mouth; but thou shalt meditate therein day and night, that thou mayest observe to do according to all that is written therein: for then thou shalt make thy way prosperous, and then thou shalt have good success.

ISAIAH 1:19

19 If ye be willing and obedient, ye shall eat the good of the land.

Overcomer's Confession:

I will be obedient to God's Word and His plan for my life. Therefore, I will eat the good of the land!

OFFENSES

*An act that causes anger, resentment,
displeasure, or affront.*

NEW TESTAMENT

ACTS 24:16

16 And herein do I exercise myself, to have always
a conscience void of offence toward God, and
toward men.

MATTHEW 18:7

7 Woe unto the world because of offences! for it
must needs be that offences come; but woe to
that man by whom the offence cometh!

JOHN 16:1 (*Amplified*)

1 I have told you all these things, so that you
should not be offended (taken unawares and
falter, or be caused to stumble and fall away).
[I told you to keep you from being scandalized
and repelled.]

1 CORINTHIANS 10:31,32

31 Whether therefore ye eat, or drink, or whatsoever ye do, do all to the glory of God.
32 Give none offence, neither to the Jews, nor to
the Gentiles, nor to the church of God.

2 CORINTHIANS 6:1,3

1   We then, as workers together with him, beseech
    you also that ye receive not the grace of God in
    vain . . . .
3   Giving no offence in any thing, that the min-
    istry be not blamed.

2 CORINTHIANS 12:20 (*NIV*)

20 For I am afraid that when I come I may not find
    you as I want you to be, and you may not find
    me as you want me to be. I fear that there may
    be quarreling, jealousy, outbursts of anger, fac-
    tions, slander, gossip, arrogance and disorder.

EPHESIANS 4:31

31 Let all bitterness, and wrath, and anger, and
    clamour, and evil speaking, be put away from
    you, with all malice.

JAMES 1:19,20

19 Wherefore, my beloved brethren, let every man
    be swift to hear, slow to speak, slow to wrath:
20 For the wrath of man worketh not the righteous-
    ness of God.

OLD TESTAMENT

PSALM 37:8

8 Cease from anger, and forsake wrath: fret not thyself in any wise to do evil.

PROVERBS 12:16 (*NIV*)

16 A fool shows his annoyance at once, but a prudent man overlooks an insult.

PSALM 119:165 (*Amplified*)

165 Great peace have they who love Your law; nothing shall offend them or make them stumble.

PROVERBS 14:29 (*NIV*)

29 A patient man has great understanding, but a quick-tempered man displays folly.

Overcomer's Confession:

I will not be offended by others, and I'll be careful not to do the offending. I walk in love and overcome offenses.

OPPRESSION

A feeling of being immovably weighed down,
as with worries or problems;
physical or mental distress.

NEW TESTAMENT

MATTHEW 23:2-4

2   Saying, The scribes and the Pharisees sit in Moses' seat:

3   All therefore whatsoever they bid you observe, that observe and do; but do not ye after their works: for they say, and do not.

4   For they bind heavy burdens and grievous to be borne, and lay them on men's shoulders; but they themselves will not move them with one of their fingers.

JAMES 2:5,6

5   Hearken, my beloved brethren, Hath not God chosen the poor of this world rich in faith, and heirs of the kingdom which he hath promised to them that love him?

6   But ye have despised the poor. Do not rich men oppress you, and draw you before the judgment seats?

OLD TESTAMENT

DEUTERONOMY 23:15,16

15 Thou shalt not deliver unto his master the servant which is escaped from his master unto thee:

16 He shall dwell with thee, even among you, in that place which he shall choose in one of thy gates, where it liketh him best: thou shalt not oppress him.

DEUTERONOMY 24:14,15

14 Thou shalt not oppress an hired servant that is poor and needy, whether he be of thy brethren, or of thy strangers that are in thy land within thy gates:

15 At his day thou shalt give him his hire, neither shall the sun go down upon it; for he is poor, and setteth his heart upon it: lest he cry against thee unto the Lord, and it be sin unto thee.

PSALM 9:9

9 The Lord also will be a refuge for the oppressed, a refuge in times of trouble.

PSALM 12:5 (*NIV*)

5 "Because of the oppression of the weak and the groaning of the needy, I will now arise," says

the Lord. "I will protect them from those who malign them."

Psalm 119:134

134 Deliver me from the oppression of man: so will I keep thy precepts.

Proverbs 22:22

22 Rob not the poor, because he is poor: neither oppress the afflicted in the gate.

Proverbs 14:31 (*NIV*)

31 He who oppresses the poor shows contempt for their Maker, but whoever is kind to the needy honors God.

Isaiah 54:14

14 In righteousness shalt thou be established: thou shalt be far from oppression; for thou shalt not fear: and from terror; for it shall not come near thee.

Overcomer's Confession:

Oppression is far from me. I am free in Jesus' Name!

P

PATIENCE

*The will or ability to wait or endure
without complaint.*

NEW TESTAMENT

ROMANS 2:6,7 (*Amplified*)

6 For He will render to every man according to
his works [justly, as his deeds deserve]:

7 To those who by patient persistence in well-
doing [springing from piety] seek [unseen but
sure] glory and honor and [the eternal blessed-
ness of] immortality, He will give eternal life.

ROMANS 5:2-4

2 By whom [Jesus] also we have access by faith
into this grace wherein we stand, and rejoice in
hope of the glory of God.

3 And not only so, but we glory in tribulations
also: knowing that tribulation worketh patience;

4 And patience, experience; and experience, hope.

GALATIANS 6:9

9 And let us not be weary in well doing: for in due
season we shall reap, if we faint not.

EPHESIANS 4:1,2

1   I therefore, the prisoner of the Lord, beseech you that ye walk worthy of the vocation wherewith ye are called,
2   With all lowliness and meekness, with longsuffering, forbearing one another in love.

TITUS 2:1,2

1   But speak thou the things which become sound doctrine:
2   That the aged men be sober, grave, temperate, sound in faith, in charity, in patience.

HEBREWS 6:12 (*NIV*)

12 We do not want you to become lazy, but to imitate those who through faith and patience inherit what has been promised.

HEBREWS 12:1

1   Wherefore seeing we also are compassed about with so great a cloud of witnesses, let us lay aside every weight, and the sin which doth so easily beset us, and let us run with patience the race that is set before us.

OLD TESTAMENT

PSALM 37:7

7   Rest in the Lord, and wait patiently for him: fret not thyself because of him who prospereth in his way, because of the man who bringeth wicked devices to pass.

PSALM 40:1

1   I waited patiently for the Lord; and he inclined unto me, and heard my cry.

LAMENTATIONS 3:26,27 (*Amplified*)

26 It is good that one should hope in and wait quietly for the salvation (the safety and ease) of the Lord.
27 It is good for a man that he should bear the yoke [of divine disciplinary dealings] in his youth.

Overcomer's Confession:

Thank You, Lord, for helping me walk in patience. I will be patient and kind today.

PEACE

Freedom from strife, contention, and mental conflict; harmony; tranquillity.

NEW TESTAMENT

JOHN 14:27 (*Amplified*)

27 Peace I leave with you; My [own] peace I now give and bequeath to you. Not as the world gives do I give to you. Do not let your hearts be troubled, neither let them be afraid. [Stop allowing yourselves to be agitated and disturbed; and do not permit yourselves to be fearful and intimidated and cowardly and unsettled.]

LUKE 1:78,79

78 Through the tender mercy of our God; whereby the dayspring from on high hath visited us,
79 To give light to them that sit in darkness and in the shadow of death, to guide our feet into the way of peace.

JOHN 16:33

33 These things I have spoken unto you, that in me ye might have peace. In the world ye shall have tribulation: but be of good cheer; I have overcome the world.

ACTS 10:36 (*NIV*)

36 You know the message God sent to the people of Israel, telling the good news of peace through Jesus Christ, who is Lord of all.

ROMANS 5:1 (*Amplified*)

1 Therefore, since we are justified (acquitted, declared righteous, and given a right standing with God) through faith, let us [grasp the fact that we] have [the peace of reconciliation to hold and to enjoy] peace with God through our Lord Jesus Christ (the Messiah, the Anointed One).

ROMANS 8:6 (*Amplified*)

6 Now the mind of the flesh [which is sense and reason without the Holy Spirit] is death [death that comprises all the miseries arising from sin, both here and hereafter]. But the mind of the [Holy] Spirit is life and [soul] peace [both now and forever].

ROMANS 14:17

17 For the kingdom of God is not meat and drink; but righteousness, and peace, and joy in the Holy Ghost.

EPHESIANS 2:14-17

14 For he [Jesus] is our peace, who hath made both one, and hath broken down the middle wall of partition between us;
15 Having abolished in his flesh the enmity, even the law of commandments contained in ordinances; for to make in himself of twain one new man, so making peace;
16 And that he might reconcile both unto God in one body by the cross, having slain the enmity thereby:
17 And came and preached peace to you which were afar off, and to them that were nigh.

OLD TESTAMENT

PSALM 4:8

8 I will both lay me down in peace, and sleep: for thou, Lord, only makest me dwell in safety.

PSALM 25:12,13

12 What man is he that feareth the Lord? him shall he teach in the way that he shall choose.
13 His soul shall dwell at ease; and his seed shall inherit the earth.

PSALM 29:11

11 The Lord will give strength unto his people; the Lord will bless his people with peace.

PROVERBS 3:24

24 When thou liest down, thou shalt not be afraid: yea, thou shalt lie down, and thy sleep shall be sweet.

ISAIAH 9:6

6 For unto us a child is born, unto us a son is given: and the government shall be upon his shoulder: and his name shall be called Wonderful, Counsellor, The mighty God, The everlasting Father, The Prince of Peace.

ISAIAH 26:3

3 Thou wilt keep him in perfect peace, whose mind is stayed on thee: because he trusteth in thee.

ISAIAH 54:10

10 For the mountains shall depart, and the hills be removed; but my kindness shall not depart from thee, neither shall the covenant of my peace be removed, saith the Lord that hath mercy on thee.

Overcomer's Confession:

I am keeping my mind on God today. Nothing can steal my peace. I have the peace of God that passes all understanding.

Q

QUARRELS

An angry disagreement or dispute.

NEW TESTAMENT

COLOSSIANS 3:12,13

12 Put on therefore, as the elect of God, holy and beloved, bowels of mercies, kindness, humbleness of mind, meekness, longsuffering;

13 Forbearing one another, and forgiving one another, if any man have a quarrel against any: even as Christ forgave you, so also do ye.

ACTS 15:39

39 And the contention was so sharp between them [Paul and Barnabus], that they departed asunder one from the other: and so Barnabas took Mark, and sailed unto Cyprus.

ROMANS 13:13

13 Let us walk honestly, as in the day; not in rioting and drunkenness, not in chambering and wantonness, not in strife and envying.

1 THESSALONIANS 2:2 (*Amplified*)

2   But though we had already suffered and been outrageously treated at Philippi, as you know, yet in [the strength of] our God we summoned courage to proclaim to you unfalteringly the good news (the Gospel) with earnest contention and much conflict and great opposition.

OLD TESTAMENT

PSALM 31:20

20   Thou shalt hide them in the secret of thy presence from the pride of man: thou shalt keep them secretly in a pavilion from the strife of tongues.

PROVERBS 13:10 (*NIV*)

10   Pride only breeds quarrels, but wisdom is found in those who take advice.

PROVERBS 17:14

14   The beginning of strife is as when one letteth out water: therefore leave off contention, before it be meddled with.

PROVERBS 20:3

3   It is an honour for a man to cease from strife: but every fool will be meddling.

PROVERBS 25:8 (*Amplified*)

8   Rush not forth soon to quarrel [before magis-
     trates or elsewhere], lest you know not what to
     do in the end when your neighbor has put you
     to shame.

Overcomer's Confession:

I will not be argumentative nor allow harsh words
to come out of my mouth. I walk in the love of God.

QUITTING

To abandon; forsake; give up; resign.

NEW TESTAMENT

2 CORINTHIANS 4:8,9

8   We are troubled on every side, yet not distressed; we are perplexed, but not in despair;

9   Persecuted, but not forsaken; cast down, but not destroyed.

2 CORINTHIANS 4:16,17

16 For which cause we faint not; but though our outward man perish, yet the inward man is renewed day by day.

17 For our light affliction, which is but for a moment, worketh for us a far more exceeding and eternal weight of glory.

GALATIANS 6:9

9   And let us not be weary in well doing: for in due season we shall reap, if we faint not.

JOHN 17:4

4   I have glorified thee on the earth: I have finished the work which thou gavest me to do.

PHILIPPIANS 3:13,14 (*NIV*)

13 Brothers, I do not consider myself yet to have taken hold of it. But one thing I do: Forgetting what is behind and straining toward what is ahead,

14 I press on toward the goal to win the prize for which God has called me heavenward in Christ Jesus.

2 TIMOTHY 4:7

7 I have fought a good fight, I have finished my course, I have kept the faith.

HEBREWS 10:23-25

23 Let us hold fast the profession of our faith without wavering; (for he is faithful that promised;)

24 And let us consider one another to provoke unto love and to good works:

25 Not forsaking the assembling of ourselves together, as the manner of some is; but exhorting one another: and so much the more, as ye see the day approaching.

HEBREWS 13:5

5 Let your conversation be without covetousness; and be content with such things as ye have: for he hath said, I will never leave thee, nor forsake thee.

OLD TESTAMENT

JOSHUA 24:16

16 And the people answered and said, God forbid that we should forsake the Lord, to serve other gods.

JUDGES 2:12

12 And they forsook the Lord God of their fathers, which brought them out of the land of Egypt, and followed other gods, of the gods of the people that were round about them, and bowed themselves unto them, and provoked the Lord to anger.

1 SAMUEL 8:8

8   According to all the works which they have done since the day that I brought them up out of Egypt even unto this day, wherewith they have forsaken me, and served other gods, so do they also unto thee.

1 KINGS 8:57

57 The Lord our God be with us, as he was with our fathers: let him not leave us, nor forsake us.

NEHEMIAH 9:31

31 Nevertheless for thy great mercies' sake thou
   didst not utterly consume them, nor forsake
   them; for thou art a gracious and merciful God.

Overcomer's Confession:

I will not quit because God is on my side!

R

REBELLION

Opposition to rightful authority;
an open show of defiance.

NEW TESTAMENT

HEBREWS 3:7,8 (*Amplified*)

7 Therefore, as the Holy Spirit says: Today, if you will hear His voice,

8 Do not harden your hearts, as [happened] in the rebellion [of Israel] and their provocation and embitterment [of Me] in the day of testing in the wilderness.

JUDE 1:11 (*NIV*)

11 Woe to them! They [the wicked] have taken the way of Cain; they have rushed for profit into Balaam's error; they have been destroyed in Korah's rebellion.

ROMANS 10:21 (*NIV*)

21 But concerning Israel he says, "All day long I have held out my hands to a disobedient and obstinate people."

TITUS 1:9-11 (*NIV*)

9 He [an overseer] must hold firmly to the trust-worthy message as it has been taught, so that he can encourage others by sound doctrine and refute those who oppose it.
10 For there are many rebellious people, mere talkers and deceivers, especially those of the circumcision group.
11 They must be silenced, because they are ruin-ing whole households by teaching things they ought not to teach — and that for the sake of dishonest gain.

TITUS 2:9 (*Amplified*)

9 [Tell] bond servants to be submissive to their masters, to be pleasing and give satisfaction in every way. [Warn them] not to talk back or con-tradict.

OLD TESTAMENT

1 SAMUEL 15:23

23 For rebellion is as the sin of witchcraft, and stubbornness is as iniquity and idolatry. Because thou hast rejected the word of the Lord, he hath also rejected thee from being king.

NEHEMIAH 9:16,17

16 But they and our fathers dealt proudly, and hardened their necks, and hearkened not to thy commandments,

17 And refused to obey, neither were mindful of
   thy wonders that thou didst among them; but
   hardened their necks, and in their rebellion
   appointed a captain to return to their bondage:
   but thou art a God ready to pardon, gracious
   and merciful, slow to anger, and of great kindness, and forsookest them not.

PROVERBS 17:11

11 An evil man seeketh only rebellion: therefore a
   cruel messenger shall be sent against him.

ISAIAH 30:8,9

8 Now go, write it before them in a table, and note
   it in a book, that it may be for the time to come
   for ever and ever:
9 That this is a rebellious people, lying children,
   children that will not hear the law of the Lord.

Overcomer's Confession:

I will not harden my heart to God's voice when He
tells me what to do. I'm faithful to do His will and
obey His Word.

Repentance

Regret or sorrow for transgressions committed;
a complete reversal of one's attitude,
behavior or values.

NEW TESTAMENT

1 John 1:9 (*Amplified*)

9   If we [freely] admit that we have sinned and
    confess our sins, He is faithful and just (true to
    His own nature and promises) and will forgive
    our sins [dismiss our lawlessness] and [contin-
    uously] cleanse us from all unrighteousness
    [everything not in conformity to His will in
    purpose, thought, and action].

Matthew 3:1,2

1   In those days came John the Baptist, preaching
    in the wilderness of Judaea,
2   And saying, Repent ye: for the kingdom of
    heaven is at hand.

Hebrews 12:15-17

15 Looking diligently lest any man fail of the grace
    of God; lest any root of bitterness springing up
    trouble you, and thereby many be defiled;

16 Lest there be any fornicator, or profane person, as Esau, who for one morsel of meat sold his birthright.
17 For ye know how that afterward, when he would have inherited the blessing, he was rejected: for he found no place of repentance, though he sought it carefully with tears.

MATTHEW 9:13

13 But go ye and learn what that meaneth, I will have mercy, and not sacrifice: for I am not come to call the righteous, but sinners to repentance.

ACTS 2:38

38 Then Peter said unto them, Repent, and be baptized every one of you in the name of Jesus Christ for the remission of sins, and ye shall receive the gift of the Holy Ghost.

ACTS 3:19 (NIV)

19 Repent, then, and turn to God, so that your sins may be wiped out, that times of refreshing may come from the Lord.

ROMANS 2:3,4 (NIV)

3 So when you, a mere man, pass judgment on them and yet do the same things, do you think you will escape God's judgment?

4   Or do you show contempt for the riches of his kindness, tolerance and patience, not realizing that God's kindness leads you toward repentance?

OLD TESTAMENT

2 CHRONICLES 7:14 (*Amplified*)

14   If my people, who are called by My name, shall humble themselves, pray, seek, crave, and require of necessity My face and turn from their wicked ways, then will I hear from heaven, forgive their sin, and heal their land.

NEHEMIAH 1:9

9   But if ye turn unto me, and keep my commandments, and do them; though there were of you cast out unto the uttermost part of the heaven, yet will I gather them from thence, and will bring them unto the place that I have chosen to set my name there.

PROVERBS 28:13

13   He that covereth his sins shall not prosper: but whoso confesseth and forsaketh them shall have mercy.

ISAIAH 55:6 (*Amplified*)

6   Seek, inquire for, and require the Lord while
    He may be found [claiming Him by necessity
    and by right]; call upon Him while He is near.

Overcomer's Confession:

When I stumble, I will immediately confess my sin
to God and forsake my wrong ways. I will do whatever is necessary to maintain unbroken fellowship
with the Lord.

RIGHTEOUSNESS

*The ability to stand before a holy God
without the sense of guilt or inferiority,
as though sin never existed.*

NEW TESTAMENT

2 CORINTHIANS 5:21

21 For he [God] hath made him [Jesus] to be sin for
us, who knew no sin; that we might be made the
righteousness of God in him.

MATTHEW 6:33 (*Amplified*)

33 But seek (aim at and strive after) first of all
His kingdom and His righteousness (His way of
doing and being right), and then all these
things taken together will be given you besides.

ROMANS 4:3,13

3 For what saith the scripture? Abraham
believed God, and it was counted unto him for
righteousness . . . .

13 For the promise, that he should be the heir of
the world, was not to Abraham, or to his seed,
through the law, but through the righteousness
of faith.

ROMANS 4:20-22

20 He [Abraham] staggered not at the promise of God through unbelief; but was strong in faith, giving glory to God;

21 And being fully persuaded that, what he had promised, he was able also to perform.

22 And therefore it was imputed to him for righteousness.

ROMANS 14:17

17 For the kingdom of God is not meat and drink; but righteousness, and peace, and joy in the Holy Ghost.

2 CORINTHIANS 9:10 (*NIV*)

10 Now he who supplies seed to the sower and bread for food will also supply and increase your store of seed and will enlarge the harvest of your righteousness.

<u>OLD TESTAMENT</u>

GENESIS 15:3-6

3 And Abram said, Behold, to me thou hast given no seed: and, lo, one born in my house is mine heir.

4 And, behold, the word of the Lord came unto him, saying, This shall not be thine heir; but he

that shall come forth out of thine own bowels shall be thine heir.

5   And he brought him forth abroad, and said, Look now toward heaven, and tell the stars, if thou be able to number them: and he said unto him, So shall thy seed be.

6   And he believed in the Lord; and he counted it to him for righteousness.

DEUTERONOMY 6:25

25 And it shall be our righteousness, if we observe to do all these commandments before the Lord our God, as he hath commanded us.

JOB 29:14

14 I put on righteousness, and it clothed me: my judgment was as a robe and a diadem.

PSALM 17:15

15 As for me, I will behold thy face in righteousness: I shall be satisfied, when I awake, with thy likeness.

PROVERBS 13:6 (*NIV*)

6   Righteousness guards the man of integrity, but wickedness overthrows the sinner.

Proverbs 21:21

21 He that followeth after righteousness and mercy findeth life, righteousness, and honour.

Isaiah 32:17

17 And the work of righteousness shall be peace; and the effect of righteousness quietness and assurance for ever.

Overcomer's Confession:

Because of the blood of Jesus, I stand righteous in God's sight. And as I seek after God's Kingdom and His way of doing and being right, all my needs are met!

S

SIN

Intentional or unintentional disobedience to the will of God.

NEW TESTAMENT

ROMANS 3:23,24

23 For all have sinned, and come short of the glory of God;

24 Being justified freely by his grace through the redemption that is in Christ Jesus.

ROMANS 5:12

12 Wherefore, as by one man sin entered into the world, and death by sin; and so death passed upon all men, for that all have sinned.

ROMANS 6:11-14

11 Likewise reckon ye also yourselves to be dead indeed unto sin, but alive unto God through Jesus Christ our Lord.

12 Let not sin therefore reign in your mortal body, that ye should obey it in the lusts thereof.

13 Neither yield ye your members as instruments of unrighteousness unto sin: but yield yourselves unto God, as those that are alive from the

dead, and your members as instruments of righteousness unto God.
14 For sin shall not have dominion over you: for ye
are not under the law, but under grace.

JAMES 1:13-15 (*NIV*)

13 When tempted, no one should say, "God is
tempting me." For God cannot be tempted by
evil, nor does he tempt anyone;
14 but each one is tempted when, by his own evil
desire, he is dragged away and enticed.
15 Then, after desire has conceived, it gives birth
to sin; and sin, when it is full-grown, gives
birth to death.

JAMES 2:10,11 (*NIV*)

10 For whoever keeps the whole law and yet stum-
bles at just one point is guilty of breaking all of
it.
11 For he who said, "Do not commit adultery," also
said, "Do not murder." If you do not commit
adultery but do commit murder, you have
become a lawbreaker.

1 JOHN 3:4

4 Whosoever committeth sin transgresseth also
the law: for sin is the transgression of the law.

OLD TESTAMENT

PSALM 51:1-3

1   Have mercy upon me, O God, according to thy lovingkindness: according unto the multitude of thy tender mercies blot out my transgressions.
2   Wash me throughly from mine iniquity, and cleanse me from my sin.
3   For I acknowledge my transgressions: and my sin is ever before me.

PROVERBS 24:8,9

8   He that deviseth to do evil shall be called a mischievous person.
9   The thought of foolishness is sin: and the scorner is an abomination to men.

ECCLESIASTES 5:6 (*NIV*)

6   Do not let your mouth lead you into sin. And do not protest to the [temple] messenger, "My vow was a mistake." Why should God be angry at what you say and destroy the work of your hands?

ISAIAH 1:18,19

18 Come now, and let us reason together, saith the Lord: though your sins be as scarlet, they shall

be as white as snow; though they be red like crimson, they shall be as wool.

19 If ye be willing and obedient, ye shall eat the good of the land.

Overcomer's Confession:

By the blood of Jesus, my sins are washed away. Now I refuse to let sin have dominion over me!

SMOKING

To inhale and exhale smoke from a cigarette, cigar, or pipe.

NEW TESTAMENT

PHILIPPIANS 4:13 (*Amplified*)

13 I have strength for all things in Christ Who empowers me [I am ready for anything and equal to anything through Him Who infuses inner strength into me; I am self-sufficient in Christ's sufficiency].

ROMANS 4:17 (*NIV*)

17 As it is written: "I have made you [Abraham] a father of many nations." He is our father in the sight of God, in whom he believed — the God who gives life to the dead and calls things that are not as though they were.

1 CORINTHIANS 3:16,17

16 Know ye not that ye are the temple of God, and that the Spirit of God dwelleth in you?
17 If any man defile the temple of God, him shall God destroy; for the temple of God is holy, which temple ye are.

2 CORINTHIANS 6:16,17

16 And what agreement hath the temple of God with idols? for ye are the temple of the living God; as God hath said, I will dwell in them, and walk in them; and I will be their God, and they shall be my people.

17 Wherefore come out from among them, and be ye separate, saith the Lord, and touch not the unclean thing; and I will receive you.

1 CORINTHIANS 6:12 (*Amplified*)

12 Everything is permissible (allowable and lawful) for me; but not all things are helpful (good for me to do, expedient and profitable when considered with other things). Everything is lawful for me, but I will not become the slave of anything or be brought under its power.

ROMANS 6:5-7

5 For if we have been planted together in the likeness of his [Jesus'] death, we shall be also in the likeness of his resurrection:

6 Knowing this, that our old man is crucified with him, that the body of sin might be destroyed, that henceforth we should not serve sin.

7 For he that is dead is freed from sin.

LUKE 4:18,19

18 The Spirit of the Lord is upon me, because he hath anointed me to preach the gospel to the poor; he hath sent me to heal the broken-hearted, to preach deliverance to the captives, and recovering of sight to the blind, to set at liberty them that are bruised,

19 To preach the acceptable year of the Lord.

OLD TESTAMENT

PSALM 32:7

7 Thou art my hiding place; thou shalt preserve me from trouble; thou shalt compass me about with songs of deliverance. Selah.

PSALM 116:16 (*NIV*)

16 O Lord, truly I am your servant; I am your servant, the son of your maidservant; you have freed me from my chains.

Overcomer's Confession:

I will not be a slave to the habit of smoking. I call those things that be not as though they are; therefore, I am a non-smoker. Thank You, Lord, for setting me free!

STRIFE

Heated dispute; hostile conflict; a skirmish,
fray, or argument.

NEW TESTAMENT

MATTHEW 5:25

25 Agree with thine adversary quickly, whiles thou art in the way with him; lest at any time the adversary deliver thee to the judge, and the judge deliver thee to the officer, and thou be cast into prison.

MATTHEW 5:39-41 (*NIV*)

39 But I tell you, Do not resist an evil person. If someone strikes you on the right cheek, turn to him the other also.
40 And if someone wants to sue you and take your tunic, let him have your cloak as well.
41 If someone forces you to go one mile, go with him two miles.

ROMANS 12:18

18 If it be possible, as much as lieth in you, live peaceably with all men.

1 CORINTHIANS 3:3,4

3 For ye are yet carnal: for whereas there is among you envying, and strife, and divisions, are ye not carnal, and walk as men?

4 For while one saith, I am of Paul; and another, I am of Apollos; are ye not carnal?

PHILIPPIANS 2:3

3 Let nothing be done through strife or vainglory; but in lowliness of mind let each esteem other better than themselves.

OLD TESTAMENT

GENESIS 13:8,9

8 And Abram said unto Lot, Let there be no strife, I pray thee, between me and thee, and between my herdmen and thy herdmen; for we be brethren.

9 Is not the whole land before thee? separate thyself, I pray thee, from me: if thou wilt take the left hand, then I will go to the right; or if thou depart to the right hand, then I will go to the left.

PROVERBS 10:12

12 Hatred stirreth up strifes: but love covereth all sins.

PROVERBS 13:10 (*Amplified*)

10 By pride and insolence comes only contention, but with the well-advised is skillful and godly Wisdom.

PROVERBS 15:18

18 A wrathful man stirreth up strife: but he that is slow to anger appeaseth strife.

PROVERBS 26:17

17 He that passeth by, and meddleth with strife belonging not to him, is like one that taketh a dog by the ears.

PROVERBS 26:20

20 Where no wood is, there the fire goeth out: so where there is no talebearer, the strife ceaseth.

Overcomer's Confession:

As far as is possible with me, I will pursue peace with others. Because of the love of God inside me, I will stop strife before it has a chance to start!

T

TEMPERANCE

*Moderation and self-restraint,
as in behavior or expression.*

NEW TESTAMENT

ROMANS 13:14

14 But put ye on the Lord Jesus Christ, and make not provision for the flesh, to fulfil the lusts thereof.

1 CORINTHIANS 9:25-27

25 And every man that striveth for the mastery is temperate in all things. Now they do it to obtain a corruptible crown; but we an incorruptible.

26 I therefore so run, not as uncertainly; so fight I, not as one that beateth the air:

27 But I keep under my body, and bring it into subjection: lest that by any means, when I have preached to others, I myself should be a castaway.

GALATIANS 5:22,23

22 But the fruit of the Spirit is love, joy, peace, longsuffering, gentleness, goodness, faith,

23 Meekness, temperance: against such there is
    no law.

PHILIPPIANS 4:5

5   Let your moderation be known unto all men.
    The Lord is at hand.

2 PETER 1:5,6

5   And beside this, giving all diligence, add to
    your faith virtue; and to virtue knowledge;
6   And to knowledge temperance; and to temper-
    ance patience; and to patience godliness.

OLD TESTAMENT

PROVERBS 23:1,2 (*NIV*)

1   When you sit to dine with a ruler, note well
    what is before you,
2   and put a knife to your throat if you are given
    to gluttony.

PROVERBS 25:16 (*NIV*)

16 If you find honey, eat just enough — too much
    of it, and you will vomit.

Overcomer's Confession:

I will yield to the force of temperance that resides
within me. By the power of the Holy Spirit, I am
moderate and self-controlled in all things!

TEMPTATION

Anything that entices one to commit sin.

NEW TESTAMENT

MATTHEW 26:41 *(Amplified)*

41 All of you must keep awake (give strict attention, be cautious and active) and watch and
pray, that you may not come into temptation.
The spirit indeed is willing, but the flesh is
weak.

MATTHEW 4:1

1   Then was Jesus led up of the Spirit into the
wilderness to be tempted of the devil.

ROMANS 12:21

21 Be not overcome of evil, but overcome evil with
good.

1 CORINTHIANS 10:13

13 There hath no temptation taken you but such as
is common to man: but God is faithful, who will
not suffer you to be tempted above that ye are
able; but will with the temptation also make a
way to escape, that ye may be able to bear it.

EPHESIANS 6:11,12

11 Put on the whole armour of God, that ye may be able to stand against the wiles of the devil.

12 For we wrestle not against flesh and blood, but against principalities, against powers, against the rulers of the darkness of this world, against spiritual wickedness in high places.

1 TIMOTHY 6:9,10 (*NIV*)

9 People who want to get rich fall into temptation and a trap and into many foolish and harmful desires that plunge men into ruin and destruction.

10 For the love of money is a root of all kinds of evil. Some people, eager for money, have wandered from the faith and pierced themselves with many griefs.

HEBREWS 4:15 (*Amplified*)

15 For we do not have a High Priest Who is unable to understand and sympathize and have a shared feeling with our weaknesses and infirmities and liability to the assaults of temptation, but One Who has been tempted in every respect as we are, yet without sinning.

JAMES 1:2,3

2 My brethren, count it all joy when ye fall into divers temptations;

3   Knowing this, that the trying of your faith worketh patience.

OLD TESTAMENT

GENESIS 39:7-12

7   And it came to pass after these things, that his
master's wife cast her eyes upon Joseph; and
she said, Lie with me.
8   But he refused, and said unto his master's wife,
Behold, my master wotteth not what is with
me in the house, and he hath committed all
that he hath to my hand;
9   There is none greater in this house than I; neither hath he kept back any thing from me but
thee, because thou art his wife: how then can I
do this great wickedness, and sin against God?
10 And it came to pass, as she spake to Joseph day
by day, that he hearkened not unto her, to lie by
her, or to be with her.
11 And it came to pass about this time, that Joseph
went into the house to do his business; and
there was none of the men of the house there
within.
12 And she caught him by his garment, saying, Lie
with me: and he left his garment in her hand,
and fled, and got him out.

PROVERBS 1:10

10 My son, if sinners entice thee, consent thou not.

PROVERBS 4:14,15

14 Enter not into the path of the wicked, and go not in the way of evil men.
15 Avoid it, pass not by it, turn from it, and pass away.

PROVERBS 16:29

29 A violent man enticeth his neighbour, and leadeth him into the way that is not good.

Overcomer's Confession:

I will not yield to the temptations that devil puts in my path. God has provided a way of escape so I can obey Him every time!

U

UNBELIEF (*see* DOUBT)

*Lack of faith, trust, or confidence,
especially in religious matters.*

NEW TESTAMENT

MATTHEW 17:14-18

14 And when they were come to the multitude,
there came to him [Jesus] a certain man,
kneeling down to him, and saying,

15 Lord, have mercy on my son: for he is lunatick,
and sore vexed: for ofttimes he falleth into the
fire, and oft into the water.

16 And I brought him to thy disciples, and they
could not cure him.

17 Then Jesus answered and said, O faithless and
perverse generation, how long shall I be with
you? how long shall I suffer you? bring him
hither to me.

18 And Jesus rebuked the devil; and he departed
out of him: and the child was cured from that
very hour.

MARK 16:15,16

15 And he [Jesus] said unto them, Go ye into all
the world, and preach the gospel to every creature.

16 He that believeth and is baptized shall be saved; but he that believeth not shall be damned.

LUKE 8:11,12

11 Now the parable is this: The seed is the word of God.

12 Those by the way side are they that hear; then cometh the devil, and taketh away the word out of their hearts, lest they should believe and be saved.

JOHN 8:23,24

23 And he [Jesus] said unto them [the Jews], Ye are from beneath; I am from above: ye are of this world; I am not of this world.

24 I said therefore unto you, that ye shall die in your sins: for if ye believe not that I am he, ye shall die in your sins.

ROMANS 3:3 (*NIV*)

3 What if some did not have faith? Will their lack of faith nullify God's faithfulness?

ROMANS 4:18-20

18 Who [Abraham] against hope believed in hope, that he might become the father of many nations, according to that which was spoken, So shall thy seed be.

19 And being not weak in faith, he considered not his own body now dead, when he was about an hundred years old, neither yet the deadness of Sarah's womb:

20 He staggered not at the promise of God through unbelief; but was strong in faith, giving glory to God.

HEBREWS 3:12

12 Take heed, brethren, lest there be in any of you an evil heart of unbelief, in departing from the living God.

HEBREWS 3:17-19

17 But with whom was he grieved forty years? was it not with them that had sinned, whose carcases fell in the wilderness?

18 And to whom sware he that they should not enter into his rest, but to them that believed not?

19 So we see that they could not enter in because of unbelief.

OLD TESTAMENT

NUMBERS 20:12

12 And the Lord spake unto Moses and Aaron, Because ye believed me not, to sanctify me in the eyes of the children of Israel, therefore ye

shall not bring this congregation into the land which I have given them.

PSALM 78:19-22

19 Yea, they [the Israelites] spake against God; they said, Can God furnish a table in the wilderness?

20 Behold, he smote the rock, that the waters gushed out, and the streams overflowed; can he give bread also? can he provide flesh for his people?

21 Therefore the Lord heard this, and was wroth: so a fire was kindled against Jacob, and anger also came up against Israel;

22 Because they believed not in God, and trusted not in his salvation.

PSALM 78:32,33

32 For all this they sinned still, and believed not for his wondrous works.

33 Therefore their days did he consume in vanity, and their years in trouble.

Overcomer's Confession:

I refuse to be robbed by the thief of unbelief. I will enter my promised land of God's blessings because I'm a believer, not a doubter!

UNDERSTANDING

*To discern and comprehend the meaning
of a given idea.*

NEW TESTAMENT

EPHESIANS 5:15-17 (*Amplified*)

15 Look carefully then how you walk! Live purposefully and worthily and accurately, not as the unwise and witless, but as wise (sensible, intelligent people).

16 Making the very most of the time (buying up each opportunity], because the days are evil.

17 Therefore do not be vague and thoughtless and foolish, but understanding and firmly grasping what the will of the Lord is.

MATTHEW 15:15-18

15 Then answered Peter and said unto him, Declare unto us this parable.

16 And Jesus said, Are ye also yet without understanding?

17 Do not ye yet understand, that whatsoever entereth in at the mouth goeth into the belly, and is cast out into the draught?

18 But those things which proceed out of the mouth come forth from the heart; and they defile the man.

LUKE 24:45

45 Then opened he [Jesus] their [the disciples']
understanding, that they might understand the
scriptures.

1 CORINTHIANS 14:14,15

14 For if I pray in an unknown tongue, my spirit
prayeth, but my understanding is unfruitful.
15 What is it then? I will pray with the spirit, and
I will pray with the understanding also: I will
sing with the spirit, and I will sing with the
understanding also.

EPHESIANS 1:15-18

15 Wherefore I also, after I heard of your faith in
the Lord Jesus, and love unto all the saints,
16 Cease not to give thanks for you, making men-
tion of you in my prayers;
17 That the God of our Lord Jesus Christ, the
Father of glory, may give unto you the spirit of
wisdom and revelation in the knowledge of him:
18 The eyes of your understanding being enlight-
ened; that ye may know what is the hope of his
calling, and what the riches of the glory of his
inheritance in the saints.

PHILIPPIANS 4:7

7 And the peace of God, which passeth all understanding, shall keep your hearts and minds through Christ Jesus.

MATTHEW 13:12,13 (*NIV*)

12 Whoever has will be given more, and he will have an abundance. Whoever does not have, even what he has will be taken from him.

13 This is why I speak to them in parables: "Though seeing, they do not see; though hearing, they do not hear or understand."

OLD TESTAMENT

EXODUS 31:2,3

2 See, I have called by name Bezaleel the son of Uri, the son of Hur, of the tribe of Judah:

3 And I have filled him with the spirit of God, in wisdom, and in understanding, and in knowledge, and in all manner of workmanship.

EXODUS 36:1

1 Then wrought Bezaleel and Aholiab, and every wise hearted man, in whom the Lord put wisdom and understanding to know how to work all manner of work for the service of the sanctuary, according to all that the Lord had commanded.

1 KINGS 3:9,11,12

9   Give therefore thy servant [Solomon] an understanding heart to judge thy people, that I may discern between good and bad: for who is able to judge this thy so great a people? . . .

11 And God said unto him, Because thou hast asked this thing, and hast not asked for thyself long life; neither hast asked riches for thyself, nor hast asked the life of thine enemies; but hast asked for thyself understanding to discern judgment;

12 Behold, I have done according to thy words: lo, I have given thee a wise and an understanding heart . . . .

PSALM 32:9

9   Be ye not as the horse, or as the mule, which have no understanding: whose mouth must be held in with bit and bridle, lest they come near unto thee.

PSALM 49:3

3   My mouth shall speak of wisdom; and the meditation of my heart shall be of understanding.

PSALM 119:34

34 Give me understanding, and I shall keep thy law; yea, I shall observe it with my whole heart.

PSALM 119:99

99 I have more understanding than all my teach-
ers: for thy testimonies are my meditation.

PROVERBS 1:5

5 A wise man will hear, and will increase learning;
and a man of understanding shall attain unto
wise counsels.

Overcomer's Confession:

My heart is quick to understand God's ways and
His Word. I walk through this life with purpose
and accuracy, firmly grasping God's will for my life!

V

VANITY

Any thing or act that is futile, idle, or worthless.

NEW TESTAMENT

1 TIMOTHY 6:20 (*Amplified*)

20 O Timothy, guard and keep the deposit
entrusted [to you]! Turn away from the irrever-
ent babble and godless chatter, with the vain
and empty and worldly phrases, and the sub-
tleties and the contradictions in what is falsely
called knowledge and spiritual illumination.

1 CORINTHIANS 3:20-23

20 And again, The Lord knoweth the thoughts of the
wise, that they are vain.

21 Therefore let no man glory in men. For all things
are yours;

22 Whether Paul, or Apollos, or Cephas, or the
world, or life, or death, or things present, or
things to come; all are yours;

23 And ye are Christ's; and Christ is God's.

1 TIMOTHY 1:5,6 (*Amplified*)

5 Whereas the object and purpose of our instruction and charge is love, which springs from a

pure heart and a good (clear) conscience and sincere (unfeigned) faith.

6   But certain individuals have missed the mark on this very matter and have wandered away into vain arguments and discussions and purposeless talk.

2 TIMOTHY 2:16

16 But shun profane and vain babblings: for they will increase unto more ungodliness.

TITUS 3:9

9   But avoid foolish questions, and genealogies, and contentions, and strivings about the law; for they are unprofitable and vain.

ACTS 14:15

15 And [Paul and Barnabus] saying, Sirs, why do ye these things? We also are men of like passions with you, and preach unto you that ye should turn from these vanities unto the living God, which made heaven, and earth, and the sea, and all things that are therein.

OLD TESTAMENT

2 KINGS 17:14,15

14 Notwithstanding they [Israel and Judah] would not hear, but hardened their necks, like to the

neck of their fathers, that did not believe in the
Lord their God.

15 And they rejected his statutes, and his covenant
that he made with their fathers, and his testimonies which he testified against them; and
they followed vanity, and became vain, and went
after the heathen that were round about them,
concerning whom the Lord had charged them,
that they should not do like them.

PSALM 4:2 (*Amplified*)

2 O you sons of men, how long will you turn my
honor and glory into shame? How long will you
love vanity and futility and seek after lies?
Selah [pause and calmly think of that]!

PSALM 12:1-3

1 Help, Lord; for the godly man ceaseth; for the
faithful fail from among the children of men.
2 They speak vanity every one with his neighbour:
with flattering lips and with a double heart do
they speak.
3 The Lord shall cut off all flattering lips, and the
tongue that speaketh proud things.

Overcomer's Confession:

I will not seek after vain and worthless things that
lead to ungodliness. I'll guard the Word that is in
my heart.

VENGEANCE

*Infliction of punishment in return
for a wrong committed; retribution.*

NEW TESTAMENT

ROMANS 12:17-19 (*NIV*)

17 Do not replay anyone evil for evil. Be careful to
do what is right in the eyes of everybody.

18 If it is possible, as far as it depends on you, live
at peace with everyone.

19 Do not take revenge, my friends, but leave room
for God's wrath, for it is written: "It is mine to
avenge; I will repay," says the Lord.

1 THESSALONIANS 5:15

15 See that none render evil for evil unto any man;
but ever follow that which is good, both among
yourselves, and to all men.

1 PETER 3:9 (*Amplified*)

9 Never return evil for evil or insult for insult
(scolding, tongue-lashing, berating), but on the
contrary blessing [praying for their welfare,
happiness, and protection, and truly pitying
and loving them]. For know that to this you
have been called, that you may yourselves
inherit a blessing [from God — that you may

obtain a blessing as heirs, bringing welfare and happiness and protection].

1 PETER 2:23 (*NIV*)

23 When they hurled their insults at him [Jesus], he did not retaliate; when he suffered, he made no threats. Instead, he entrusted himself to him who judges justly.

LUKE 9:54,55

54 And when his [Jesus'] disciples James and John saw this, they said, Lord, wilt thou that we command fire to come down from heaven, and consume them, even as Elias did?

55 But he turned, and rebuked them, and said, Ye know not what manner of spirit ye are of.

OLD TESTAMENT

LEVITICUS 19:18

18 Thou shalt not avenge, nor bear any grudge against the children of thy people, but thou shalt love thy neighbour as thyself: I am the Lord.

PROVERBS 24:29

29 Say not, I will do so to him as he hath done to me: I will render to the man according to his work.

EZEKIEL 25:15-17 (*NIV*)

15 "This is what the Sovereign Lord says: 'Because the Philistines acted in vengeance and took revenge with malice in their hearts, and with ancient hostility sought to destroy Judah,

16 therefore this is what the Sovereign Lord says: I am about to stretch out my hand against the Philistines, and I will cut off the Kerethites and destroy those remaining along the coast.

17 I will carry out great vengeance on them and punish them in my wrath. Then they will know that I am the Lord, when I take vengeance on them.'"

Overcomer's Confession:

I never return evil for evil nor insult for insult. Instead, I entrust myself to my Heavenly Father who judges righteously. I depend on Him to uphold my cause.

VICTORY

*Success in any contest or struggle
involving the defeat of an opponent
or the overcoming of obstacles.*

NEW TESTAMENT

2 CORINTHIANS 2:14 (*Amplified*)

14 But thanks be to God, Who in Christ always leads us in triumph [as trophies of Christ's victory] and through us spreads and makes evident the fragrance of the knowledge of God everywhere.

ROMANS 8:37-39

37 Nay, in all these things we are more than conquerors through him that loved us.
38 For I am persuaded, that neither death, nor life, nor angels, nor principalities, nor powers, nor things present, nor things to come,
39 Nor height, nor depth, nor any other creature, shall be able to separate us from the love of God, which is in Christ Jesus our Lord.

JOHN 16:33

33 These things I have spoken unto you, that in me ye might have peace. In the world ye shall have

tribulation: but be of good cheer; I have overcome the world.

ROMANS 12:21

21 Be not overcome of evil, but overcome evil with good.

1 JOHN 2:14

14 I have written unto you, fathers, because ye have known him that is from the beginning. I have written unto you, young men, because ye are strong, and the word of God abideth in you, and ye have overcome the wicked one.

1 JOHN 4:4

4 Ye are of God, little children, and have overcome them: because greater is he that is in you, than he that is in the world.

1 JOHN 5:4 (*Amplified*)

4 For whatever is born of God is victorious over the world; and this is the victory that conquers the world, even our faith.

REVELATION 2:7

7 He that hath an ear, let him hear what the Spirit saith unto the churches; To him that

overcometh will I give to eat of the tree of life, which is in the midst of the paradise of God.

OLD TESTAMENT

EXODUS 15:1,2

1 Then sang Moses and the children of Israel this song unto the Lord, and spake, saying, I will sing unto the Lord, for he hath triumphed gloriously: the horse and his rider hath he thrown into the sea.

2 The Lord is my strength and song, and he is become my salvation: he is my God, and I will prepare him an habitation; my father's God, and I will exalt him.

NUMBERS 13:30

30 And Caleb stilled the people before Moses, and said, Let us go up at once, and possess it; for we are well able to overcome it.

PSALM 41:11,12

11 By this I know that thou favourest me, because mine enemy doth not triumph over me.

12 And as for me, thou upholdest me in mine integrity, and settest me before thy face for ever.

Psalm 47:1

1   O clap your hands, all ye people; shout unto
    God with the voice of triumph.

Psalm 98:1

1   O sing unto the Lord a new song; for he hath
    done marvellous things: his right hand, and his
    holy arm, hath gotten him the victory.

Overcomer's Confession:

Thank You, Lord, that You always lead me in victory
as I follow You and obey Your Word. Greater is He
who is in me than he that is in the world!

W

WEAKNESS

*An inability to produce results; the state
or quality of being powerless.*

NEW TESTAMENT

2 CORINTHIANS 12:9

9   And he [the Lord] said unto me [Paul], My
grace is sufficient for thee: for my strength is
made perfect in weakness. Most gladly therefore will I rather glory in my infirmities, that
the power of Christ may rest upon me.

MATTHEW 26:41

41 Watch and pray, that ye enter not into temptation: the spirit indeed is willing, but the flesh is
weak.

ROMANS 5:5,6

5   And hope maketh not ashamed; because the
love of God is shed abroad in our hearts by the
Holy Ghost which is given unto us.

6   For when we were yet without strength, in due
time Christ died for the ungodly.

205

ROMANS 8:26,27 (*NIV*)

26 In the same way, the Spirit helps us in our weakness. We do not know what we ought to pray for, but the Spirit himself intercedes for us with groans that words cannot express.

27 And he who searches our hearts knows the mind of the Spirit, because the Spirit intercedes for the saints in accordance with God's will.

1 CORINTHIANS 9:22 (*NIV*)

22 To the weak I became weak, to win the weak. I have become all things to all men so that by all possible means I might save some.

1 CORINTHIANS 12:21,22

21 And the eye cannot say unto the hand, I have no need of thee: nor again the head to the feet, I have no need of you.

22 Nay, much more those members of the body, which seem to be more feeble, are necessary.

1 JOHN 4:4

4 Ye are of God, little children, and have overcome them: because greater is he that is in you, than he that is in the world.

OLD TESTAMENT

PSALM 46:1

1 God is our refuge and strength, a very present help in trouble.

JOEL 3:9,10

9 Proclaim ye this among the Gentiles; Prepare war, wake up the mighty men, let all the men of war draw near; let them come up:

10 Beat your plowshares into swords, and your pruninghooks into spears: let the weak say, I am strong.

ISAIAH 35:3,4

3 Strengthen ye the weak hands, and confirm the feeble knees.

4 Say to them that are of a fearful heart, Be strong, fear not: behold, your God will come with vengeance, even God with a recompence; he will come and save you.

Overcomer's Confession:

The Greater One in me gives me strength. I am strong! I am strong! I am strong!

WIFE (*see* HUSBAND)

*A woman with reference to the man
to whom she is married.*

NEW TESTAMENT

EPHESIANS 5:22,23

22 Wives, submit yourselves unto your own husbands, as unto the Lord.

23 For the husband is the head of the wife, even as Christ is the head of the church: and he is the saviour of the body.

1 CORINTHIANS 7:2 (*Amplified*)

2 But because of the temptation to impurity and to avoid immorality, let each [man] have his own wife and let each [woman] have her own husband.

1 CORINTHIANS 7:15,16

15 But if the unbelieving depart, let him depart. A brother or a sister is not under bondage in such cases: but God hath called us to peace.

16 For what knowest thou, O wife, whether thou shalt save thy husband? or how knowest thou, O man, whether thou shalt save thy wife?

1 CORINTHIANS 11:3

3 But I would have you know, that the head of every man is Christ; and the head of the woman is the man; and the head of Christ is God.

1 CORINTHIANS 11:11,12 (*NIV*)

11 In the Lord, however, woman is not independent of man, nor is man independent of woman.

12 For as woman came from man, so also man is born of woman. But everything comes from God.

EPHESIANS 5:31

31 For this cause shall a man leave his father and mother, and shall be joined unto his wife, and they two shall be one flesh.

COLOSSIANS 3:18

18 Wives, submit yourselves unto your own husbands, as it is fit in the Lord.

1 TIMOTHY 3:11

11 Even so must their [the deacons'] wives be grave, not slanderers, sober, faithful in all things.

1 TIMOTHY 5:14 (*NIV*)

14 So I counsel younger widows to marry, to have
    children, to manage their homes and to give the
    enemy no opportunity for slander.

1 PETER 3:1-5

1 Likewise, ye wives, be in subjection to your own
   husbands; that, if any obey not the word, they
   also may without the word be won by the conversation of the wives;
2 While they behold your chaste conversation
   coupled with fear.
3 Whose adorning let it not be that outward
   adorning of plaiting the hair, and of wearing of
   gold, or of putting on of apparel;
4 But let it be the hidden man of the heart, in that
   which is not corruptible, even the ornament of a
   meek and quiet spirit, which is in the sight of
   God of great price.
5 For after this manner in the old time the holy
   women also, who trusted in God, adorned themselves, being in subjection unto their own husbands.

OLD TESTAMENT

GENESIS 2:18 (*Amplified*)

18 Now the Lord God said, It is not good (sufficient,
    satisfactory) that the man should be alone; I will

make him a helper meet (suitable, adapted, complementary) for him.

PROVERBS 12:4

4 A virtuous woman is a crown to her husband: but she that maketh ashamed is as rottenness in his bones.

PROVERBS 18:22

22 Whoso findeth a wife findeth a good thing, and obtaineth favour of the Lord.

PROVERBS 31:10-12 (*NIV*)

10 A wife of noble character who can find? She is worth far more than rubies.
11 Her husband has full confidence in her and lacks nothing of value.
12 She brings him good, not harm, all the days of her life.

Overcomer's Confession:

[Women:] I am a wife of noble character. I honor and respect my husband, bringing him good and not harm all the days of my life!

[Men:] My wife is a woman of noble character, I have full confidence in her ability to bring me good and not harm all the days of my life!

WISDOM

*Comprehension of what is true, just, or enduring;
the ability to judge rightly and follow the soundest
course of action based on knowledge,
experience, and understanding.*

NEW TESTAMENT

MATTHEW 7:24,25

24 Therefore whosoever heareth these sayings of mine, and doeth them, I will liken him unto a wise man, which built his house upon a rock:

25 And the rain descended, and the floods came, and the winds blew, and beat upon that house; and it fell not: for it was founded upon a rock.

JOHN 7:17

17 If any man will do his will, he shall know of the doctrine, whether it be of God, or whether I speak of myself.

JOHN 8:32

32 And ye shall know the truth, and the truth shall make you free.

ACTS 6:10

10 And they [certain Jews] were not able to resist the wisdom and the spirit by which he [Stephen] spake.

ROMANS 16:19 (*NIV*)

19 Everyone has heard about your obedience, so I am full of joy over you; but I want you to be wise about what is good, and innocent about what is evil.

1 CORINTHIANS 2:6 (*Amplified*)

6 Yet when we are among the full-grown (spiritually mature Christians who are ripe in understanding), we do impart a [higher] wisdom (the knowledge of the divine plan previously hidden); but it is indeed not a wisdom of this present age or of this world nor of the leaders and rulers of this age, who are being brought to nothing and are doomed to pass away.

1 CORINTHIANS 3:18

18 Let no man deceive himself. If any man among you seemeth to be wise in this world, let him become a fool, that he may be wise.

2 CORINTHIANS 2:11

11 Lest Satan should get an advantage of us: for we are not ignorant of his devices.

EPHESIANS 5:15

15 See then that ye walk circumspectly, not as fools, but as wise.

OLD TESTAMENT

PSALM 111:10

10 The fear of the Lord is the beginning of wisdom: a good understanding have all they that do his commandments: his praise endureth for ever.

PROVERBS 2:7

7   He layeth up sound wisdom for the righteous: he is a buckler to them that walk uprightly.

PROVERBS 4:7

7   Wisdom is the principal thing; therefore get wisdom: and with all thy getting get understanding.

PROVERBS 8:11

11 For wisdom is better than rubies; and all the things that may be desired are not to be compared to it.

PROVERBS 10:8 (*NIV*)

8   The wise in heart accept commands, but a chattering fool comes to ruin.

PROVERBS 10:13,14

13 In the lips of him that hath understanding wisdom is found: but a rod is for the back of him that is void of understanding.
14 Wise men lay up knowledge: but the mouth of the foolish is near destruction.

PROVERBS 12:15

15 The way of a fool is right in his own eyes: but he that hearkeneth unto counsel is wise.

PROVERBS 16:23

23 The heart of the wise teacheth his mouth, and addeth learning to his lips.

Overcomer's Confession:

I walk in the wisdom of God because I have planted the Word of God in my heart. I have made it my top priority to get God's wisdom and then to live it!

WORDS

Something spoken; an proclamation,
a statement, or a remark.

NEW TESTAMENT

MATTHEW 12:36,37

36 But I say unto you, That every idle word that men shall speak, they shall give account thereof in the day of judgment.

37 For by thy words thou shalt be justified, and by thy words thou shalt be condemned.

JOHN 6:63

63 It is the spirit that quickeneth; the flesh profiteth nothing: the words that I [Jesus] speak unto you, they are spirit, and they are life.

JOHN 6:67,68

67 Then said Jesus unto the twelve, Will ye also go away?

68 Then Simon Peter answered him, Lord, to whom shall we go? thou hast the words of eternal life.

EPHESIANS 4:29 (*NIV*)

29 Do not let any unwholesome talk come out of your mouths, but only what is helpful for building

others up according to their needs, that it may benefit those who listen.

EPHESIANS 5:6

6 Let no man deceive you with vain words: for because of these things cometh the wrath of God upon the children of disobedience.

COLOSSIANS 4:6

6 Let your speech be alway with grace, seasoned with salt, that ye may know how ye ought to answer every man.

2 TIMOTHY 2:14 (*NIV*)

14 Keep reminding them of these things. Warn them before God against quarreling about words; it is of no value, and only ruins those who listen.

JAMES 1:19

19 Wherefore, my beloved brethren, let every man be swift to hear, slow to speak, slow to wrath.

JAMES 3:8-10

8 But the tongue can no man tame; it is an unruly evil, full of deadly poison.

9   Therewith bless we God, even the Father; and therewith curse we men, which are made after the similitude of God.

10 Out of the same mouth proceedeth blessing and cursing. My brethren, these things ought not so to be.

OLD TESTAMENT

PROVERBS 6:2

2   Thou art snared with the words of thy mouth, thou art taken with the words of thy mouth.

PROVERBS 15:23 (*Amplified*)

23 A man has joy in making an apt answer, and a word spoken at the right moment — how good it is!

PROVERBS 18:21

21 Death and life are in the power of the tongue: and they that love it shall eat the fruit thereof.

PROVERBS 25:11

11 A word fitly spoken is like apples of gold in pictures of silver.

PROVERBS 29:20

20 Seest thou a man that is hasty in his words? there is more hope of a fool than of him.

ECCLESIASTES 10:12

12 The words of a wise man's mouth are gracious;
but the lips of a fool will swallow up himself.

ISAIAH 50:4

4 The Lord God hath given me the tongue of the
learned, that I should know how to speak a
word in season to him that is weary: he wakeneth morning by morning, he wakeneth mine
ear to hear as the learned.

Overcomer's Confession:

I speak only words of life that build others up according to their needs. And because my words line up
with God's Word, I eat the fruit of joy and peace!

X

XENOPHOBIA

The state of being timid or disdainful of that which is alien, especially of strangers or foreign people.

AUTHOR'S NOTE: This is the only word I could think of for the letter "X"! (smile)

NEW TESTAMENT

MATTHEW 25:35 (*NIV*)

35 [Jesus will say,] "For I was hungry and you gave me something to eat, I was thirsty and you gave me something to drink, I was a stranger and you invited me in."

MATTHEW 25:43-45 (*NIV*)

43 [Jesus will say,] "I was a stranger and you did not invite me in, I needed clothes and you did not clothe me, I was sick and in prison and you did not look after me."

44 They also will answer, "Lord, when did we see you hungry or thirsty or a stranger or needing clothes or sick or in prison, and did not help you?"

45 He will reply, "I tell you the truth, whatever you did not do for one of the least of these, you did not do for me."

HEBREWS 13:1,2

1 Let brotherly love continue.
2 Be not forgetful to entertain strangers: for thereby some have entertained angels unawares.

OLD TESTAMENT

LEVITICUS 25:35-38

35 And if thy brother be waxen poor, and fallen in decay with thee; then thou shalt relieve him: yea, though he be a stranger, or a sojourner; that he may live with thee.
36 Take thou no usury of him, or increase: but fear thy God; that thy brother may live with thee.
37 Thou shalt not give him thy money upon usury, nor lend him thy victuals for increase.
38 I am the Lord your God, which brought you forth out of the land of Egypt, to give you the land of Canaan, and to be your God.

DEUTERONOMY 10:18,19 (*NIV*)

18 He defends the cause of the fatherless and the widow, and loves the alien, giving him food and clothing.
19 And you are to love those who are aliens, for you yourselves were aliens in Egypt.

DEUTERONOMY 23:7

7 Thou shalt not abhor an Edomite; for he is thy brother: thou shalt not abhor an Egyptian; because thou wast a stranger in his land.

EXODUS 22:21

21 Thou shalt neither vex a stranger, nor oppress him: for ye were strangers in the land of Egypt.

LEVITICUS 19:33,34

33 And if a stranger sojourn with thee in your land, ye shall not vex him.
34 But the stranger that dwelleth with you shall be unto you as one born among you, and thou shalt love him as thyself; for ye were strangers in the land of Egypt: I am the Lord your God.

Overcomer's Confession:

I look for ways to be a blessing to others, including those I do not know.

Y

YOUTH

The period of life between adolescence and adulthood.

NEW TESTAMENT

1 TIMOTHY 4:12

12 Let no man despise thy youth; but be thou an example of the believers, in word, in conversation, in charity, in spirit, in faith, in purity.

2 TIMOTHY 2:22

22 Flee also youthful lusts: but follow righteousness, faith, charity, peace, with them that call on the Lord out of a pure heart.

TITUS 2:6 (*NIV*)

6 Similarly, encourage the young men to be self-controlled.

GALATIANS 4:1,2

1 Now I say, That the heir, as long as he is a child, differeth nothing from a servant, though he be lord of all;
2 But is under tutors and governors until the time appointed of the father.

ACTS 2:38,39

38 Then Peter said unto them, Repent, and be baptized every one of you in the name of Jesus Christ for the remission of sins, and ye shall receive the gift of the Holy Ghost.

39 For the promise is unto you, and to your children, and to all that are afar off, even as many as the Lord our God shall call.

EPHESIANS 6:4

4 And, ye fathers, provoke not your children to wrath: but bring them up in the nurture and admonition of the Lord.

MATTHEW 15:5,6

5 But ye say, Whosoever shall say to his father or his mother, It is a gift, by whatsoever thou mightest be profited by me;

6 And honour not his father or his mother, he shall be free. Thus have ye made the commandment of God of none effect by your tradition.

1 JOHN 2:14

14 I have written unto you, fathers, because ye have known him that is from the beginning. I have written unto you, young men, because ye are strong, and the word of God abideth in you, and ye have overcome the wicked one.

OLD TESTAMENT

PROVERBS 15:5

5   A fool despiseth his father's instruction: but he that regardeth reproof is prudent.

PROVERBS 28:7

7   Whoso keepeth the law is a wise son: but he that is a companion of riotous men shameth his father.

PROVERBS 20:11

11 Even a child is known by his doings, whether his work be pure, and whether it be right.

Overcomer's Confession:

[Youth:] I am strong in the Lord and have overcome the wicked one because the Word of God abides in me. I follow after righteousness, faith, love, and peace while I am still young.

Z

ZEAL

*Fervent dedication to a purpose or a goal and
a steadfast diligence in its advancement.*

NEW TESTAMENT

MATTHEW 11:12 (*Amplified*)

12 And from the days of John the Baptist until the
present time, the kingdom of heaven has
endured violent assault, and violent men seize it
by force [as a precious prize — a share in the
heavenly kingdom is sought with most ardent
zeal and intense exertion].

MATTHEW 5:13-16

13 Ye are the salt of the earth: but if the salt have
lost his savour, wherewith shall it be salted? it is
thenceforth good for nothing, but to be cast out,
and to be trodden under foot of men.

14 Ye are the light of the world. A city that is set on
an hill cannot be hid.

15 Neither do men light a candle, and put it under a
bushel, but on a candlestick; and it giveth light
unto all that are in the house.

16 Let your light so shine before men, that they may
see your good works, and glorify your Father
which is in heaven.

LUKE 22:32,33

32 But I [Jesus] have prayed for thee [Peter], that thy faith fail not: and when thou art converted, strengthen thy brethren.

33 And he said unto him, Lord, I am ready to go with thee, both into prison, and to death.

1 CORINTHIANS 14:12

12 Even so ye, forasmuch as ye are zealous of spiritual gifts, seek that ye may excel to the edifying of the church.

1 CORINTHIANS 15:58

58 Therefore, my beloved brethren, be ye stedfast, unmoveable, always abounding in the work of the Lord, forasmuch as ye know that your labour is not in vain in the Lord.

GALATIANS 6:9

9 And let us not be weary in well doing: for in due season we shall reap, if we faint not.

TITUS 2:14

14 Who gave himself for us, that he might redeem us from all iniquity, and purify unto himself a peculiar people, zealous of good works.

REVELATION 3:19 (*Amplified*)

19 Those whom I [dearly and tenderly] love, I tell their faults and convict and convince and reprove and chasten [I discipline and instruct them]. So be enthusiastic and in earnest and burning with zeal and repent [changing your mind and attitude].

ROMANS 10:2,3 (*NIV*)

2 For I can testify about them [Israel] that they are zealous for God, but their zeal is not based on knowledge.

3 Since they did not know the righteousness that comes from God and sought to establish their own, they did not submit to God's righteousness.

OLD TESTAMENT

JOSHUA 24:15

15 And if it seem evil unto you to serve the Lord, choose you this day whom ye will serve; whether the gods which your fathers served that were on the other side of the flood, or the gods of the Amorites, in whose land ye dwell: but as for me and my house, we will serve the Lord.

EZRA 7:23 (*NIV*)

23 "Whatever is commanded by the God of heaven, let it be done with zeal for the house of the God of heaven, lest there be wrath against the kingdom of the king and his sons."

PSALM 119:139,140

139 My zeal hath consumed me, because mine enemies have forgotten thy words.
140 Thy word is very pure: therefore thy servant loveth it.

Overcomer's Confession:

I go after the things of God with fervent zeal. I am zealous of good works, zealous of spiritual gifts, and zealous to repent of anything that keeps me from obtaining my precious prize. The zeal of God has consumed me!

PRAYER FOR SALVATION

God cares for you and wants to help you overcome in every area of your life. That's why He sent Jesus to die for you.

If you have never received Jesus Christ as your personal Savior, you can make your heart right with God this very moment. In doing so, you will make Heaven your eternal home.

Pray this prayer from your heart:

> Oh, God, I ask You to forgive me of my sins. I believe You sent Jesus to die on the Cross for me. I receive Jesus Christ as my personal Savior. I confess Him as Lord of my life, and I give my life to Him. Thank You, Lord, for saving me and for making me new. In Jesus' Name, amen.

If you prayed this prayer for the first time, I want to welcome you to the family of God! Please write me at the address on the following page and let me know about your decision for Jesus. I'd like to send you some free literature to help you in your walk with the Lord.

BUILD YOUR OWN FAITH CONFESSION

_____

_____

_____

_____

_____

_____

_____

_____

_____

_____

_____

_____

_____

_____

_____

_____

_____

_____

_____

BUILD YOUR OWN FAITH CONFESSION

_____

_____

_____

_____

_____

_____

_____

_____

_____

_____

_____

_____

_____

_____

_____

_____

_____

_____

_____

_____

BUILD YOUR OWN FAITH CONFESSION

_____

_____

_____

_____

_____

_____

_____

_____

_____

_____

_____

_____

_____

_____

_____

_____

_____

_____

Build Your Own Faith Confession

_____

_____

_____

_____

_____

_____

_____

_____

_____

_____

_____

_____

_____

_____

_____

_____

_____

_____

_____

For Further Information

To receive:

- additional copies of this book,
- a complete catalog of Rev. Kate McVeigh's books and tapes,
- a free subscription to her bimonthly newsletter,
- or information regarding Kate's ministry schedule,

please write or call:

Kate McVeigh Ministries
P.O. Box 1688
Warren, MI 48090
1-810-795-8885
www.katemcveigh.org

POWER-PACKED
TEACHING MATERIALS

By Kate McVeigh

BOOKS

THE FAVOR FACTOR • $7.00

In this book, Kate provides rich teaching on the subject of supernatural favor.

You'll find out:

- What divine favor really is.

- How to release your faith for supernatural favor with God and man.

- Twenty ways to lose favor.

- How to pray for favor in various areas of life.

THE DOCTRINE OF HEALING • $1.00

This helpful minibook contains:

- Healing scriptures.

- Reasons why God wants you healed.

- Cases of healing in the Bible.

AUDIOTAPES

HEALING — GOD'S WILL FOR YOU
2-tape series — $10.00

Know beyond a shadow of a doubt that *God wants you well*!

Titles in this series include:

- God Wants You Healed
- The Word Will Work for You

HOW TO KEEP YOUR JOY
2-tape series — $10.00

Learn how to live in the joy of the Lord every day of your life!

Titles in this series include:

- How To Keep Your Joy
- Stir It Up

I AM DETERMINED
2-tape series — $10.00

If you're going to go all the way with God, you have to be determined!

Titles in this series include:

- I Am Determined — Part 1
- I Am Determined — Part 2

SUPERNATURAL FAVOR
2-tape series — $10.00

This series will teach you how to walk in continual favor with God and man.

Titles in this series include:

- Supernatural Favor
- Crowned With Favor

THE MINISTRY OF ANGELS
2-tape series — $10.00

Angels are God's messengers sent to minister on our behalf.

Titles in this series include:

- The Ministry of Angels — Part 1
- The Ministry of Angels — Part 2

THE MERCY OF GOD
3-tape series — $15.00

Learn how to tap into God's endless mercies, which are new every morning for *you*!

Titles in this series include:

- The Mercy of God
- Facing Truth and Finding Freedom
- Freedom From Guilt and Condemnation

EFFECTIVE PRAYER
4-tape series — $20.00

Learn how to receive an answer every time you pray!

Titles in this series include:

- Seven Steps to Answered Prayer
- The Lord's Prayer
- How To Pray Effectively for Others
- Ask and You Shall Receive

HAVING VICTORY OVER INTIMIDATION, INSECURITY, WORRY, AND FEAR
4-tape series — $20.00

You can learn how to walk in victory over the intimidation, insecurity, and fear the devil tries to send your way!

In this series, Kate also discusses:

- How to live in boldness.
- Overcoming insecurities.
- How to walk in the freedom to be yourself!

WALKING IN THE SPIRIT
4-tape series — $20.00

The subjects discussed in this series are vital to your spiritual health!

You will learn:

- How to overcome the flesh.
- How to get rid of bad habits.
- The rewards of self-discipline.
- How diligence produces results.

YOUR FAITH WILL MAKE YOU WHOLE
4-tape series — $20.00

Without faith, it's impossible to enjoy the abundant life God has for you.

This dynamic series teaches you:

- How to receive your healing or miracle from God.
- How your faith can make you whole in any area of life.
- How to catch the Spirit of faith.
- The principles of faith described in God's Word.

GOD'S LAWS OF FINANCIAL INCREASE
6-tape series — $30.00

If you're always struggling in the area of finances, this powerful six-tape series is for you!

Kate teaches you:

- How to increase financially.
- God's plan of prosperity for your life.

KATE MCVEIGH MINISTRIES ORDER FORM

For faster service, complete this order form and call:

1-800-40-FAITH

(Please have your Visa or MasterCard ready.)

Title	Qty. x	Price =	Ext. Price
TOTAL ORDER			$
Postage & Handling (*Please add 10%*)			
GRAND TOTAL (Payment must accompany all orders.)			$

Payment Method ☐ Cash\Check ☐ Visa ☐ MasterCard

Credit Card # __ __ __ __-__ __ __ __-__ __ __ __-__ __ __ __

Exp. Date_____ Signature_____

SOLD TO

Name

Address

City

State   Zip

Telephone (   )   FAX (   )